Following the Breadcrumbs

'What an inspiration Philippa is. Not only does she share messages of hope and God's love through her beautiful songs but also through her writing. This book will show you how much God can do for us, if we let him.'

Tim Jupp – founder of BigChurchDayOut, Delirious?

'Philippa Hanna is the real deal – not only an incredible musical talent with a genuine passion for Jesus, but now she shows a great gift as a writer too. This book will entertain, inspire, and nourish your soul. Buy it.'

Jeff Lucas – author, speaker, broadcaster

'A brilliant read. Philippa's story fairly bounces along, and I can tell you from experience that this girl and her journey of faith are absolutely for real.'

Adrian Plass – author, speaker

FOLLOWING THE BREADCRUMBS

A journey from darkness to light
through everyday miracles

PHILIPPA HANNA

Copyright © 2013 Philippa Hanna

23 22 21 20 19 18 17   10 9 8 7 6 5 4

First published 2013, reprinted 2014, 2017 by Authentic Media Limited
PO Box 6326, Bletchley, Milton Keynes, MK1 9GG.
www.authenticmedia.co.uk

British Library Cataloguing in Publication Data
A catalogue record for this book is available from the British Library.
ISBN: 978-1-78078-087-0
978-1-78078-088-7 (e-book)

Cover photography: Rosie Hardy
Cover design by Kate Swarbrick
Printed and bound by CPI Group (UK) Ltd., Croydon, CR0 4YY.

For Pat and Sandra Hanna
I didn't choose you, but given the chance,
I would have.

CONTENTS

Contents

Introduction

Does God Exist?

WHATEVER OUR 'religion' status on Facebook – Christian, Hindu, Muslim, Atheist, Jedi – most of us would surely welcome conclusive *evidence* that there is a God. I reached the age of nineteen with no real persuasion either way, until one night when one prayer changed everything. The content and intention of this book is to provide my humble case that the Truth really is out there. A Truth that surpasses fantasy. A Truth that can transform the darkest tale into the most glorious story.

There are countless dimensions to the God debate, but this book is not about the age of the universe or evolution. It's not a book about theology. What you're about to read is a collection of stories that, although they are fantastic, are all 100 per cent true. I must add at this stage that the detail of certain conversations may be slightly inaccurate. But to all ends the content is as accurate as my brain and the witness of those included can recall.

It is in essence my 'story'. My aim is to recount this journey with honesty and detail. I will testify to what I've seen, heard and felt – not only to emotional and spiritual changes, but to *truly* miraculous events too. From instances of miraculous provision, life-changing encounters and chance meetings, to divine guidance and the scattered jigsaw of my life piecing together. The results will hopefully speak for themselves.

It's up to you to whom you give glory for them. But, I am convinced that God is behind the transformation.

Of course, there are still days when I demand answers to difficult questions, days when I lose my temper with broken appliances, trains that don't leave on time and people who disappoint me. Bad things happen to the best of people, and evil often seems to triumph.

But in spite of all this, I can't deny the goodness that flooded my world after I prayed a simple prayer.

Within this collection of anecdotes – that gathered together read as a kind of novel – I'll be taking you on a journey into the place where I was lost. I'll take you along a trail of simple signs, wonders and blessings that led me out the other side. What I hope you'll see is a living God at *work* in everyday life.

An agnostic friend of mine recently said to me, 'So, your life changed. What makes you so sure it was "God" who changed it?' I gave the question some thought, and a few hours later had a rare lateral epiphany.

If a scientist added a chemical to a Petri dish and the contents turned green, it would be illogical to assume there was no relation between the two events. The scientist would, of course, need to repeat the experiment and find the same results before safely drawing that conclusion. And that's why I've invited contributions to this book from several people, all ordinary, all different, with stories similar to mine. When God was added to those lives they changed colour too. If you can't draw belief from that, it's at the very least worthy of further exploration.

I haven't always been a believer. My journey started when I was twenty, at the end of 2004. It was a pivotal time in my young life. Just hours after praying for God to show up and change things, a chain of small events began that were to shape my life into something completely new: something alive, good, exciting, adventurous and positive. These bread-crumbs of hope will be referred to as 'miracles' for the purpose of this story. You can make up your own mind.

If you would call yourself an agnostic or an atheist you might at this point be thinking 'fate threw you a bone or two. Your luck changed.' Or 'your outlook shaped your outcome'. I see sense in those viewpoints. But what I'm about to share with you paints a picture of something deeper, richer, more logical and more consistent than luck.

My life altered beyond recognition. The grey tones of life were removed and replaced by stunning technicolour. I'd love to say it's the life I've always dreamed of. But honestly, it's more. And it's far better than I could ever have dreamed of. In the past few years since I asked for God's help I've been scratching away at a buried blueprint for my perfect life. Every day it seems to make more sense than before. Every day the Polaroid focuses another degree clearer.

Since being a Christian I have kept a list of the little 'miracles'. The keeping of the list is hint number one of this book's authenticity. We all experience the odd 'coincidence' here and there. But something in the frequency and poetic nature of these changes seemed worthy of documentation. The daily rays of light that began to weave through my world struck me as tell-worthy.

A couple of months back, I did something quite unnerving for me, I went back to Wakefield, my hometown, for drinks. It's a cute northern town (technically a city thanks to the cathedral). It's quite charming, but due to its size there is a tendency to bump into everyone you've ever known throughout your school years on an average Friday night.

When last I ventured there, it's safe to say times were darker. Wakefield was where I first stumbled drunk from a bar aged thirteen with my (slightly) older friends. Armed with Wonderbras and fake ID we got up to all kinds of antics.

I did everything I could to live beyond my years and wound up with battle scars to tell the story. The trouble with going out scantily dressed and drinking more than your body weight in cider is that you attract the wrong kind of attention. I guess you could say this behaviour helped lay the foundations for a life I eventually wanted to leave behind.

If it weren't for Facebook, I doubt anyone from school would recognize me. It's a decade since I left (aged sixteen), and everything about me has altered. There's a different person under my skin. I can't tell you how conscious I was of this fact as I graced the dance floor of one of my old haunts. Looking around, it was strange to see that it looked exactly the same as I remembered, almost as if no time had passed – the same décor, same playlist. The only difference was that people now smoked outside instead of on the dance floor.

I bumped into Mark, an old classmate. He was a clever, witty lad I'd always liked at school. We used to sit near each other in English. He recognized me straight away.

'Hey, I know you. Yeah, yeah, you used to sit next to me in English.' I began to beam and bubble, excited to catch up on the last five years. He didn't seem quite so excited. He began to say something about how I dumped him after two days in Year 11 and really hurt his feelings. 'I'm sorry,' I said with a big smile.

'I'm really sorry.' He changed the subject as I reeled from the reminder. Had I really done that? Didn't seem like me. Guess I must have been having a bad week. It had all but disappeared from my mind. Funny how certain things stay with you and others don't. I guess for him this was a sticky memory.

'So anyway I hear you're into all that God stuff now anyway?' The very tone of the question put me into preaching gear. I could tell he wasn't 'into it' like I was.

'Err, yeah I became a Christian, yeah.' From here a can of worms erupted as a pink slithery fountain. He began to tell me how atheism was his religion. He was passionate about it. He had found a pro-atheist website that inspired him more than any Christian had ever managed to. He lapped up everything atheists had to say about the stupidity of Christians.

His opening argument was, 'You were always clever, man. How can someone clever believe in an imaginary old man that lives in the sky?' I couldn't help but be flattered that he thought I was 'clever' at school. He went on, raising all of the common questions about faith. It reminded me of how I used to mock the RE teacher at school.

We'd studied all the major religions in RE. We also learned about atheism. It was a well-established movement. Atheists believed all sorts of things about God: God the public sedative; God the emotional crutch; the tradition, the fairy tale, and so on. Mark thought God to be nothing more than a figment of my post-high-school imagination.

'My life has changed Mark. It's totally transformed,' I testified professionally.

'But how do you know it's not just *you* doing the work? Give yourself some credit! You've changed your own life.' I shrugged, considering his statement. Why was I so convinced that God was involved?

'Mark, I've tried other ways to change my life. I've explored other beliefs and nothing's ever done me any *real* good. When I asked God into my life I really began to change.' This was my key argument. I'd really played my ace with that one.

'Yeah, but maybe you've just found something that works for you.' Hmm. Good comeback. I scratched my head, wishing I hadn't drunk that second glass of wine. Then it hit me.

'Miracles!' I offered. God makes actual *miracles* happen. You can't argue with miracles.' Mark laughed at me.

'What! Have you actually *seen* a miracle?' he asked. I racked my brain. No water into wine. No risen dead people. But God knows there have been many 'little miracles'.

'I have actually. Every day. It's the little things,' I said. My argument didn't hold up very well. Although in my heart I knew those everyday things counted, they weren't going to impress my inebriated friend.

We chatted, laughed and shook hands as I left, challenging him to come and see me play. One song can say more than a week's worth of chat. He 'politely' declined my invitation. Incidentally, the friends I went out with aren't Christians and it made me look rather fanatical to have got into this full-scale debate. Sigh.

The next morning I woke up way too early, my mind churning with this conversation. All I could hear in my mind were his words, 'How do you know?' If I was to have this conversation again what could I say differently? Where could I begin? Why *do* I believe in God? So, I pulled out my list of miracles.

Key moments and events that have helped transform my life. But before we get onto the miracles, you should really know a bit more about life before the miracles began . . .

PART 1
LOST IN THE WOODS

GETTING LOST

I HAD a good start in life. My mum is a warm and bubbly primary school teacher with a love of the arts and huge heart. My dad is an entertainer: a bona fide country and Irish crooner with a sparkle in his eyes and contagious wit.

Some of my earliest memories are of watching Dad entertain. He had a way on stage – a way of warming people. As a child hidden in the corners of social clubs or watching in the wings of cabaret venues, I would watch the faces in the audience. People from all walks of life loved him.

Like most twenty-first century families my colourful family had its share of challenges. Mum and Dad had both been married before my arrival. Mum had a girl, Alex, first time round. Dad had a boy and a girl, Stuart and Jacqui. When families come together in this manner it's not often like the Brady Bunch. It usually brings along with it some sensitive issues.

I was just trying to find things to do most of the time. I used to put on concerts for my dolls and sing into a hairbrush. I didn't have a great time at school. I loved the cosiness of the warm classroom with its home-made displays and pink-carpet story corner. But I remember it being quite lonely at times. I had a few friends but there were lots of fall-outs. Lots of sitting by myself. I guess I must have seemed a little 'different' from the other kids. I liked to dance around singing to myself and was more than happy to play alone. It made me a bit of a target for teasing.

I remember the first time I sang in front of my school friends. To my surprise and delight their eyes widened and sparkled and they asked me to sing again. I figured I must be quite good! That was until the time when the group's ringleader organized a pretend singing competition. We were taking it in turns to perform and cheer for each other. When it came to my turn they all booed. I scarpered in tears, their jibes ringing in my ears.

Please don't think at this point that I'm feeding you a sob story. I'm just trying to give you a context for what you'll read further on. From that day my confidence as a performer was, well, nil. I also began to crave one thing more than any other . . . to be liked.

This made High School even more of a minefield. Like many young girls, I gave into the plethora of pressures to fit in and have a good time. That, along with what was later diagnosed as teenage depression, led me down the wrong path. I entered my GCSE years with a whole lot of nothing to show for the years that had gone before.

At sixteen I had my first 'serious relationship'. We were best friends. By that time I was one of the 'bad girls' and he was a sensible, clever student. We were an unlikely pair but we had humour and music in common. We were young and daft. After an off-again-on-again two-year reign, we parted ways. It was a vivid and beautiful time.

Chasing Stars

JUST LIKE every young person, I was trying to make my way in the world through a twenty-first century lens. I was a wannabe pop star with a passion for music. Somewhere between chasing dreams and growing up I began to wonder what I believed about life. What was it all about? Why are we here? I didn't quite believe in God but I believed in something. I supposed there was *some* truth in every religion but I didn't think it really mattered.

After leaving school with a handful of GCSEs (I rather compromised my education to go to parties and doss around), I did what any aspiring artist would do and began auditioning for *everything*: girl bands, TV shows, artist development schemes, the lot. I was racking up debt on credit cards travelling to London for auditions and sessions. I was writing with anyone who needed a writer and paying all my own expenses. At that time I began to battle with my self-image, always feeling like the plain girl in the audition line.

At an audition for a show called *Fame Academy* I met a boy. I won't name him, but I'll call him Hugh (as he reminded me of Hugh Grant, on account of his soft voice and foppish charm). He was articulate, gentle and charming and I wound up working with him on a couple of things. One of those things was a romantic relationship. After just a couple of months I practically moved in to his shared house in Preston.

I came back to Yorkshire on weekends to play gigs in local pubs and social clubs. The relationship started well but after about a year began to 'go bad'. A culmination of our respective insecurities led to a volatile mess.

I realized after almost two years together that we were making one another thoroughly miserable, but being alone made me feel so afraid. I didn't have the courage to break free and start again.

I'd always been interested in the supernatural (thanks to my hippy sister Jacqui) and felt compelled to search deeper for answers. As things became more complicated in my life I'd been consulting tarot decks and using crystals to calm my anxiety. I just didn't feel comfortable in my skin. I hit an all-time low at the back-end of 2004. My search for a break in music was filled with disappointments and dead ends. In every corner of my world there seemed to be only shadows.

Roo

I USED to perform at an open mic night at Preston's Voodoo Lounge every Tuesday night. It was something that Hugh and I had been involved in together. I used to dread performing at that open mic night. It sounds absurd – performing was my biggest passion – yet I loathed it. I loved hearing my voice through the PA, bouncing off walls and tables, but I always assumed people weren't going to like me.

Despite spending most of the night in the toilets, I got something deeply valuable from those gigs. Until then, the stage had always represented a pressurized environment. My dad had instilled certain showman's values in me from childhood: professionalism and presentation were everything. He never missed a beat.

But the open mic night was anything but polished and that's why I loved it. The local musicians fascinated me. The girl with the blonde dreadlocks who turned up on a bicycle and bounced her head along from the doorway. The polite Bob Dylan fan that always played too hard and made his fingers bleed. The girl who dressed like a boy and sounded like Janis Joplin and Jimi Hendrix's lovechild. She was nuts. She once grabbed me in a doorway and said, 'All that matters is love and music man. Blow everything else.' Most of the open mic night regulars smoked roll-ups and drank lots of beer (including me). Every night was colourful.

I met some of my all-time favourite artists at that open mic night. One was Alex Platt, whose songs were cryptic, animated and charming. His high tenor vocals and vibrato reminded me of the late, great Jeff Buckley. The first night he got up to play, my eyes widened. 'This is a song I wrote yesterday. It's not really finished yet,' he said. I'd *never* heard a performer say anything like that before. He was young, potent and unapologetic with a feral craziness swimming in his ice-blue eyes.

Then there was Sean Redmond. His voice was also awesome – clear, direct and youthful. His guitar work was interesting too. He always played the same two amazing songs, 'Why play a bunch of songs no one's ever heard. Just play your two best ones and get out of there,' was something I believe Sean once said.

Then there was Roo. On his Voodoo Lounge debut I'd actually stayed home for once. The boys bounced in from the gig wielding their usual stack of minidiscs. Super organized and resourceful brother-duo John and Yewhan (Hugh's uni mates) would make sure we recorded the night every week. It was great for reviewing performances and comedy mistakes we'd made. Hugh and his band mates began playback with a nightcap.

'Phili this amazing guy was there tonight,' said Hugh. 'He was an insanely good guitarist and played a tambourine with his foot.' I listened to the recording of his set cross-legged in front of the hi-fi. This guy certainly was impressive. He'd taken a Justin Timberlake song and given it a Gypsy-jazz makeover, using the guitar body for percussion and flying mind-bending melodic riffs between comedy impressions of J.T. He was very talented and very funny.

I forgot all about Roo until the next Voodoo Lounge night when I saw the phenomenon for myself. He rocked up to the jam night with his friend Ric in tow.

We were briefly introduced as he signed up to play.

'I'm looking forward to hearing you,' I said.

'I'm playing with my acoustic duo tonight. It's even better!'

He was cheeky, confident and funny – almost a little cocky. When their slot came up I sat glued to the stage and leaned forward with bated breath. They sprang into action in a dynamic explosion of what can only be described as acoustic alternative metal folk (or something resembling nothing to do with any of that).

Their energy was enormous. Ric's voice was awesome. He delivered each song theatrically. Screeching, perilous high notes were effortless for him. In one set there were moments of sheer madness where the lyrics made my toes curl. It sounded crude and a little psychotic. There were also moments of purity to stir the heart.

Transfixed, legs crossed, I looked on with my chin in my hands.

'They are by far the coolest people I've ever seen,' I thought. I liked Ric, but was a little afraid to approach him, so I made a beeline for Roo after their set. I didn't want to seem too much like a groupie. I interjected casual banter and asked for his number. This was a person I wanted in my life forever. That night, our friendship began.

Roo came to every jam night over the months that followed. It was always better when he was there. One night I dared myself to ask if we could play together. He said yes without hesitation; I was amazed. Because he was so talented

I thought he'd be far too snobby to get on stage with a poppy singer like me. But he loved it. There was immediate musical chemistry and I felt certain he'd spoiled me for life. I never wanted to play without that incredible talent on stage beside me ever again.

In those days Roo was quite feisty. He wasn't a drinker or a smoker, but music was his life. It turned out that he was connected to all the above artists. In fact they'd all played together since they were kids. Roo's music spoke to me. The first time I heard his songs they carved out a little shelf in my heart forever.

One day, pondering on my musical future, I decided to give Roo a call. I wanted to ask if he'd learn some of my songs and do a few shows with me. I never imagined he'd be up for it, but he said yes straight away.

He came round to the house where I was pretty much living with Hugh. Feeling a little nervous of each other, we went down to the makeshift studio in the basement and jammed out one of my songs. I couldn't believe the magic; it just worked.

After a few weeks of knowing Roo I found out he'd become a Christian. He didn't seem like the God-squad type, so this really threw me. As friends we began to compare notes on our respective beliefs. Roo seemed to be changing before my eyes. I was a little worried – I didn't want our friendship to change. But the more he changed the more I was drawn to him.

One rainy spring morning I awoke from strange, haunting dreams to see Hugh sleeping beside me. From the moment I stepped into the shower I had a sense that that day was the beginning of the end of our relationship. Another two-year pattern was emerging. We had a blazing row that turned into tears and pleas and sorrys. After agreeing to take some space away from each other I returned home to my parents feeling heavy and hopeless.

It was a hard time. Things at home weren't perfect and I didn't want to be stuck in a rural area far away from any chance of advancing my career. When I think back to that time in my life 'heartbreak' is what comes to mind. My body was so racked with anxiety and emotion that I felt physically ill. My only joy had been in working with my new friend; my hopes were wrapped up in him. Not only was he helping revive me as a musician, but his friendship had also ignited something new in me.

Roo was becoming more and more involved in church. He often shared with me how his morals had changed. He told me he planned on waiting for the 'right woman' before he got involved with anyone and that he intended to wait for marriage before sleeping with anyone. I laughed off his resolve at first. Did people really do that nowadays? It didn't seem very rock and roll.

But when I reflected on the complications that sex had caused in my relationships, Roo's view seemed refreshing. I just didn't believe that I could have that strength of will. Waiting until marriage for sex seemed nothing short of saintly to me. When I met Roo's Christian friends they seemed like a different breed. *Holy* people. They were kind, loving, positive, gentle and seemed to observe things in me that I wasn't able to see for myself. One friend in particular made an unexpected impact on me.

The first time I met Andy Baker was in Roo's car. I had hopped in the front and had a brief conversation with him through the gap in the headrest. He seemed like a nice enough lad, if a little straight-laced. He made jokes here and there and asked lots of questions about my music. By strange coincidence he'd already heard me sing. He'd interned at a studio in Sheffield and edited my vocals years earlier.

He too was very open about his relationship with God. There was something about the way Andy talked about God that made him seem comically familiar: 'God does this' and 'God likes that'. He made God seem close in a funny way – like a pen pal.

I remember a conversation we had about purity. He explained how crossing physical boundaries with someone who wasn't your husband or wife was like cheating on your future spouse. I thought nuggets like this were hilarious at the time (not to mention completely unrealistic). I literally laughed out loud. But over time I realized that Andy was very serious. And if nothing else, it made me feel very safe around him.

He and Roo were both involved at a church in Preston called the Freedom Centre. This is where they'd become acquainted and where Roo had given his life to someone called Jesus.

Andy made every effort to involve me in social things he and his Christian friends were doing. I was most surprised to find him in the pub on several occasions. At the pub one evening we got into a heated debate.

'I am a Christian already!' I protested. I wasn't of course, but equally I wasn't about to let someone else call it.

'No you're not Philippa.'

'I am. I believe in Jesus . . . kind of.'

'Yes, but have you given your life to Jesus? Have you been filled with the Holy Spirit?' I just thought he was splitting hairs at this point (or talking religious mumbo-jumbo).

Something inside me so wanted to be in Andy's holy club. I just wasn't ready to change.

COINCIDENCES

THE MORE I spent time with these guys, the more I noticed 'good things' would happen around them, 'coincidences' if you will. The following is an account of one of those occasions.

Shortly after I'd moved back to my parents' place, Roo and I were offered an acoustic gig. It was for Bob, the label manager of Inspirit records (the dance label I was writing for at the time). I was so excited. We would get a chance to do our thing – our acoustic stuff! The guys had heard plenty of my dance records but this was different and more personal.

We travelled to High Wycombe in blistering heat. Everyone remembers their summers as being hotter than they were, but honestly, this summer day was a real face-melter. We travelled by train and shared earphones en route. We had to sit in the doorway for most of the way but it was OK; Roo's guitar by my feet made me feel like a rock star.

The gig was Bob's wedding reception. They'd married in Malta a few weeks earlier. It was a very posh garden party at the groom's parents' place. There was a free bar, hog roast and superstar DJs. The free bar got the better of me that night. The stress of the preceding weeks somehow worked its way out via some Stevie Wonder tunes and a bottomless glass of white wine.

The countless guests meant that even with the scale of house, we were assigned to the caravan. Somewhere near dawn I'd collapsed in a drunken, Motown haze on the sofa bed. I hadn't even thought to open the windows or shut the curtains.

As the sun came up, I didn't stir. I woke to find my mouth as dry as sand; I realized I was dehydrated, possibly to a near-fatal degree. Roo had survived it seemed, although he hadn't woken up yet.

I found my way over to the house where the more sensible wedding guests were brightly breakfasting in the mid-morning sun. The radiant bride approached me with a plate of pastries.

'I'm OK thanks,' I croaked, anything but OK. 'Could I have some water please?' I chugged what felt like gallons of the stuff and took some back for Roo. I realized at this point that I was more than just worse for wear. Certainly I'd overindulged, but on top of this I had swollen glands and a nasty sore throat. Through the haze I remembered that I needed, somehow, to make my way to Hale to join the family holiday later that day. Through a fog of fever and nausea I realized this was not good.

Hale is a small pocket of a town on the south coast near Devon. It was at least a six-hour journey by train. At this point I had no idea how I would even get to a station, let alone plan and endure the epic journey.

Roo and I eventually made it to the breakfast area and I tried to suck on a bagel. My glands seemed to be getting worse. It was a nasty mixture of post-alcohol haze and the shivers of a looming virus. I began to imagine whom I'd leave my iPod to, should I pass away suddenly.

Roo said a small prayer for me as we sniggered through the previous night's events: dancing outlandishly to 'Hey Ya' on the deserted dance floor at 2 a.m.

At that moment a couple came to sit with us. I guessed they were in their thirties and they had a new baby. They were surfy and cool.

'Not feeling too good today?' she asked, smiling knowingly.

'Nope. Definitely overdid it. Think I'm coming down with something too.' I swallowed and winced. 'Just can't believe I've got to find my way to Devon today.' The lady's eyes went far away for a moment.

'Where are you off to in Devon? We're on our way that way today, that's all,' she said sunnily. My spirits lifted a bit. Could this be a rope?

'I've got to get to Hale. My family is there on a holiday that's already started. I'm already in their bad books for missing the first bit.'

'We're going to Hale today,' she sang. 'We'll give you a ride, no problem, as long as you don't mind a six-week-old baby riding beside you. Paul this girl needs a lift to Hale today. Can you believe it?' I was amazed. It really did seem like a miracle.

The miracle expanded in the form of a six-week-old baby that made no sound for five hours. We made one comfort stop, which the baby slept through. I slept right beside him and was dropped off safely at my folks' campsite in time for a fish and chip tea.

ARGUING WITH CHRISTIANS

SUMMER ENDED and autumn's gallery prevailed. The events of August had been refreshing and I was finally gaining some sense of balance in myself. But as the September nights drew in, my mood lowered. It's always been a difficulty of mine. When the weather turns, I struggle to keep my spirits up. The events of the year didn't help.

One dark evening I found myself back in Preston. I'd gone to visit Roo for music practice. Afterwards, he asked if I fancied visiting Andy Baker at his halls of residence.

'Sure,' I said, hoping it would brighten the damp teatime heaviness.

We arrived at the spanking new-build and buzzed into Andy's floor. We entered to find the usual chaos of shared student accommodation with a softness I hadn't expected. It turned out that the vibrant bunch weren't fellow students, but the young people from the Freedom Centre hijacking the space. They were a good bunch of regular teenagers – most of them students – some of whom were working full-time at the church. While I first thought them a little 'white bread' I was very content to be there. It was a safe environment.

As we loafed around on the kitchen worktops the conversation naturally made its way round to God. Andy

Baker leaned against the cooker opposite me, a trendy, metal-encased Bible in hand. I felt a little sorry for him at the time (if he thought he was going to convert me by waving his hip aluminium NIV at me, he had another think coming). But I was somewhat touched by his resolve to 'save' my soul.

Others were involved in the conversation. A smiley lad known as 'Library Matt' (I don't know why) began to hear out my views.

'I totally believe that there's a God but I think he's outside the box that you put him in,' I said. They were good-humoured about my opinion.

'What do you mean exactly?' one of them asked.

'Well', I responded sharply, 'you think that God sends bad people to hell don't you?'

Matt paused.

'Erm, no not exactly. Just people who don't accept Jesus as their Lord.' Great, I thought. Perfect ammunition.

'Well, take Hitler for instance. I'm sure I could forgive Hitler. I don't feel particularly mad at Hitler right now. So, if I can forgive him why can't God – with or without Jesus?' Andy stepped in.

'Look Philippa, if God showed up in your life right now, would you believe it?' I thought about it and smugly responded, 'Huh, well yes, of course I would.'

'Well, there's no point in us arguing about it. Can we just pray for you?' I didn't want to contradict my own claim to be open-minded, so I agreed.

They gathered round me, a whole circle of Christians stretching out their arms toward me. Andy began to pray.

'God we pray that you'd reveal yourself to Philippa in a way that she recognizes.' The praying continued in this fashion, 'God we pray that you'd just do something, even right now.' At that point I froze, feeling very awkward. I half didn't want to disappoint them. Should I flail around or something? Maybe even just a flinch or two? But I wasn't brave enough to fake it. I went rigid.

Afterwards, a tall youth worker named Pete had a quiet word, 'I feel like you were guarding yourself then. Like you were shielding yourself from God getting in. I saw a big brick wall around your heart in my mind. I'm gonna keep praying that God breaks it down. You should come to the Freedom Centre sometime. I think you'd enjoy it.'

'Sure,' I said. 'By all means keep praying. If God wants to prove he's there then he's most welcome.'

Musical Adventures

ROO AND I continued on our musical adventures. There were some memorable moments. Not least the time we spent in Amsterdam.

It's probably just as well I had a good Christian by my side in Amsterdam. The place is colourful to say the least. I could hardly believe my luck when the guys from Inspirit Records suggested we go out there and play a set. A couple of their DJs had bookings. I somehow charmed a seed into their minds that they should book Roo and I as an acoustic act. It worked.

We flew on the day of the gig and arrived in Amsterdam around teatime. 'Aren't we cutting it a bit fine for the show?' I asked. But we weren't. Cities like Amsterdam don't sleep.

We checked into a kooky hotel in the heart of the red-light district. The quaint boutique B&B opened my mind to a world I'd never imagined. Every room was themed to cater for different tastes. But despite the location and the connotations there was an odd dignity to it. It was beautiful and impeccably kept. I figured a hotel with a dozen brothels surrounding it was safe and classy by comparison.

The gig was just around the corner in the surreal ambience of 'The Supper Club'. Dressed in our best we entered this odd parallel universe where nightclubs are clinical white bedrooms. It was more an alternative dining experience than a club. Not a sticky floor or a tacky strobe in sight.

The ground level was where all the action seemed to be taking place. A crisp white bed formed a border around the room, gleaming and spotless. My eyes struggled to focus in the dim lighting as I tried to ascertain whether the club was dodgy. My ignorant view of Amsterdam was that you should expect to find a drug-fuelled orgy in every corner. But, like our hotel, it seemed to have no seedy agenda. Why would it? Enough venues in the capital had that covered. I marvelled at my own locationism. Not all Dutch clubs were harems after all.

Smartly dressed groups grazed posh nibbles and sipped cocktails by candlelight. The only thing that made The Supper Club a club was the music. A splay of clean white speakers perched in every corner singing the smooth bass-lines and sparkling high-hats of chilled house music. This was soon to be interrupted by Roo and me playing our acoustic set. I shuddered insecurely.

The club was quite modest in size. A single table ran the length of the room and at the end was the bar where hurried bartenders collected armfuls of angular dishes. Impressively, the staff were hopping up onto the bar to distribute dishes to the top floor. A simple bed border with handrail-free staircases led to either side. British health and safety would have had a field day.

We were seated at the table and served an eccentric three-course meal. I didn't recognize a single ingredient. It was like alien seafood. Roo and I chatted to the DJs, not really knowing what was going on. Which course was the main? It didn't matter really. In these early days I would get so excruciatingly nervous before singing that these fabulous experiences were always tainted by the colour of pure fear. Even the best-seasoned octopus is hard to enjoy at such times.

If we cut a few scenes from this movie, you'd find me next standing on a two-by-two table, not a step either way to play with. The makeshift platform was designed to make me visible to the upper level. I'm not sure it really worked. All I remember was belting out a very heartfelt song about a broken relationship to a bunch of tipsy rich dudes.

I woke around 1 p.m. the following day. After the late gig we ventured into the city. We turned down lots of drugs, took a walk around the hotel and saw the girls in the windows. It was a sorry sight. The lack of anxiety in the atmosphere is confusing. Everyone seems to be so at peace with the situation, but it definitely left a strange impression on me.

'Surely prostitution can't be OK? Does something being legal mean it's OK?' I thought to myself.

Steelworks

BY NOW Roo and I had a pretty good set and there were one or two songs we were keen to record.

Andy Baker was still at uni and was making an album as part of his degree. One evening he invited us down to the studio in Sheffield where he was interning. It was the very same studio where I'd done my first-ever session. Andy kept saying how amazed he was at the 'favour' bestowed on him there. He wasn't wrong. He'd been working there as a runner and the guys had rewarded him with a set of keys.

I had immediate nostalgia. As we walked into the warm embrace of Studio 2 I had flashbacks of my first time there – the first time I heard a professional recording of my voice.

I'd been taken there as an insecure seventeen-year-old girl. I was just out of school and had no plan for my life. Andrew Platts, a musician and aspiring manager, had seen me playing at Darton Gala. After catching my nervous renditions of 'Genie in a Bottle' and 'Crush' he'd wandered over to talk to my dad. The next thing I knew he was offering to manage me. His first port of call was to showcase me to the producers he knew at Steelworks studios.

I don't remember being nervous about the showcase. I just remember the lush feeling of that warm room and the sublime treat of singing into one of those awesome condenser microphones. I remember the potent longing to do it again.

It was like I'd taken studio opium and was hooked. I loved it. Having to focus on each vocal take in such detail gripped me. I learned so much. A couple of weeks later I found myself back in the warm control room. The engineer hit play and the luminous track began. The voice on the track was mine but better. Chopped up, tuned, compressed and bathed in layers of feathery fine harmony. I was overcome. It was a life-altering moment. I'd done lots of sessions after that, the highlight of which was singing backing vocals on a B-side for Emma Bunton. But time and geography distanced me from the studio. Besides, my focus had shifted onto something closer to home – getting that big break with my own songs.

Now, years later I was back. Andy Baker sat at the desk; I stood in the doorway, Roo ahead of me.

I began chatting with Andy, recounting my first time there and listening to what he'd been working on. I have to admit at that stage his music wasn't really 'my bag'. It was so Christian. But Andy was methodical and passionate and seemed able to rope people into doing just about anything.

After a couple of moments I was introduced to two other fellows in the room – Josh and Joel. I'd barely noticed them until that moment as I was so caught up in the nostalgia and studio allure. They looked young; I figured they were a few years younger than me at least. Andy mentioned they were brothers – a bass and drums combo to boot.

'Josh and Joel, Josh and Joel,' I thought. 'I'll never remember which one is which.' They seemed reserved – shy even. Later they had a jam with Roo in the live room. It had all the social ease of a blind date set up by an eager friend playing musical cupid. The atmosphere was fidgety.

'What can you play?' Roo asked. Josh's deep eyes sparkled under his long lashes.

'Anything,' he replied nonchalantly. Silent Joel nodded coolly in agreement. They began playing. I was mesmerized. Live music was still new to me. I'd watched my dad – the one-man Irish band – entertain crowds. I'd done dozens of gigs to tracks and a handful with Roo on guitar. But the chest-shaking groove of a drum kit and bass guitar was almost too much to take.

A little later when Andy had finished his session, Roo and I set up to record. The boys lingered in the control room.

We powered through our songs. Eventually we got to 'Searched For', a sentimental ballad I'd written about breaking up with Hugh. As we played that song we had a moment. Roo's spontaneous nature meant there was always energy in the songs when we played them live. We didn't even bother to write the middle eight before the session.

The take was accidentally on purpose really good. Andy mumbled something over the talkback and we went through to the control room to listen back. We knew straight away that the performance had something special about it. I didn't think it was my best-ever vocal, but it had something in it – a rawness and transparency. Even the mistakes sounded right. Andy was quite moved.

'Wow, that was really good,' he said. It was an endearing chink in Andy's armour. In spite of his British reserve he was able to express emotion at important times.

'I just wanna pray for you Philippa.' I didn't object. He laid a hand on my shoulder. Roo did the same. I recall with some clarity what Andy said.

'God wants to use you powerfully to stir emotions in people. I can see people being deeply moved and touched by what you do. Philippa I really feel you need to give your gifts to God. Because he can do more with them that you could ever do alone.'

Andy's words made me feel a little uncomfortable. I should have been excited I suppose. But to be honest I felt a little pressured. I liked the idea of some heavenly force doing marvellous things in my life. But didn't want to become Julie Andrews, lovely as she is. I didn't want to lose my identity. I hated the idea of laying down my ambitions to some invisible almighty plan. What did it all mean?

I was confused and conflicted. We went back to our lives with the CD as our only memento of the experience.

THE PRAYER

MY SEARCH for stardom was a constant ache. Like a primal instinct I had to indulge. I wasn't sure what I was aiming for. I just knew I felt unfulfilled.

If I thought about the knock-backs I'd faced, they piled up as one big stack of rejection letters. To add insult to injury, those store card and credit card debts were beginning to mount. I was no stranger to the final demand, the late-payment charge or the 'declined' tone at the cash till. My only hope it seemed was a big break, but that big break looked ever more distant.

I'd had many brushes with darkness during my twenty years. When I say darkness I mean a number of things: fear, anxiety, depression, but more literally in uncomfortable encounters with the supernatural. In my teens I had a fascination for the stuff – horoscopes, crystals and alternative therapies. It was an interest that became a desperate crutch. As I felt a deeper sense of 'lostness' I went there for comfort. My hippy sister had prescribed me a number of prayers to ascended masters and angels. I was desperate so I tried. But I found myself wandering around in confused limbo.

So, that autumn it's fair to say that the darkness had been more real than ever before. My time spent with Andy and Roo had been a beacon of hope. They always seemed spiritually secure. They didn't have all the answers to satisfy me, but they seemed safe and when Andy spoke about spiritual matters he had an authority that gave me some peace.

I couldn't help feeling like I was moving towards something new and exciting, something that might change my life for the better. A dark evening soon after, a window of opportunity drifted open.

Remember the jam night in Preston where I met Roo? Well, his acoustic buddy Ric's dad was a recording artist. Roo asked if I wanted to go to watch him perform. It so happened that Ric's dad, Godfrey, was a Christian and the local venue was, of all places, a church. In a desperate blur I got myself ready and went along for the ride.

As I walked into the room I felt totally uncomfortable. We were late and I had too much skin on show. I searched high and low for a garment that covered my shoulders and midriff to no avail. I held onto the thought that at one time I was a 'good girl' and hoped that I could tap into that part of me.

The church had all the attributes that scared me – an altar, an organ and several woven tapestries saying things like, 'Light of the world' and 'Hope of the nations'. And it had that smell, that incomparable church smell: old and musty. It gave me the shivers.

As we found our seats, Roo gave me a slightly nervous sideways smile. The concert had begun. But it soon became apparent that it wasn't a concert at all. Two full songs in people appeared to be drifting into their own little worlds; they had their eyes closed and their palms facing upwards. I was relieved to be passing for one of them, but relief gave way to awkwardness as the atmosphere moved from sombre to slightly kooky.

There were no hymn sheets and no one was playing a pipe organ. There was simply an overhead projector with song lyrics moved occasionally by a helper at the front. She was a spritely, bespectacled lady with a great figure. My attention fixed on Ric's dad singing away at the front. He played an electric guitar quite similar to the one my dad owned at the time. As he played he began to break into spontaneous phrases and melodies that the small group seemed to bounce from, adding their own melodies. I had to admit, although a humble gathering, the sound of their voices together was almost angelic.

I looked at the words lit up on the projector just like at school.

'I can do this,' I thought. 'It's just singing. I'll sing along.' I joined the pleasant chorus and felt a pinch of comfort in the sweet words, though my heart firmed up under the touch of the experience. Just when I thought I was coping there came a strange sound behind me. A lady had started to moan. I looked behind to see her swaying, trance-like with her arms in the air. I began craning for the emergency exit sign. I looked at Andy and Roo but they both seemed OK and were singing with eyes closed. I turned again to face the singer. Was he hypnotizing people? It seemed like it. But when I considered the strange places I'd been in search of spiritual peace, I concluded that this probably wasn't any more dangerous. I resolved to stay. In the midst of the chaos, Ric's dad began to sing a song about Jesus:

My troubled soul. Why so weighed down?
You were not made to bear this heavy load
Cast all your burdens upon the Lord

Jesus cares, He cares for you
Jesus cares, He cares for you
And all your worrying won't help you make it through
Cast all your burdens upon the Lord
And trust again in the promise of His love

Extract taken from the song 'Praise the Mighty Name of Jesus' by
Robert Critchley copyright © 2001 Thankyou Music*

As I listened, the words sank deep into me, lulling my disquiet. I still felt uncomfortable, freaked out by the unfamiliarity of the situation. But in those words I started to hear a simple, peaceful offer of help.

'What am I afraid of?' I wondered suddenly. I'd been to spiritual healers and had my tarot read. I'd been to night-clubs and taken substances I didn't even know the names of, and now I was afraid? It made me wonder if there really was something significant going on.

The singer kept on singing, 'Cast all your burdens upon the Lord, 'cos Jesus cares he cares for you.' At that moment, my 'burdens' hit me like a freight train. There was heavy stuff in my life: family stuff, finance stuff and stuff within that I couldn't articulate. With nothing left to lose, I embraced the sudden urge to pray.

'Jesus if you *are* there, if you are real and if it is possible to 'know' you like these guys seem to know you, then prove it. I'm so sorry I've messed everything up. I've made a real mess of things. If you can do a better job then please take over. If it's possible to start over then I want to.'

It wasn't the first time I'd looked for answers. But it was the first time I'd looked for them in Jesus.

The evening drew to a close and after tea and cake we all went home. Roo and Andy dropped me off and I went inside out of the cold. I made a warm drink and said goodnight to Mum and Dad.

I had a job interview the next day. I was going for a job as a Christmas Elf! It was time to try to pay back some of the store cards and save for Christmas. I fell asleep feeling no different from any other night.

PART 2
FINDING THE TRAIL

A New Day

I AWOKE the next morning in November 2004 feeling somehow . . . different. For the first time in many months my heart didn't race with anxiety upon waking. The usual cloud of doom that fogged up my every morning wasn't there.

Nothing had changed exactly, but I just felt better, as if I'd resolved some longstanding dispute with a family member. It felt as if a heaviness had been lifted. I felt lighter. I bounced out of bed feeling positive about my interview. It wasn't until the early afternoon so I hung out in my room for a little while. I reached for my phone. My heart would always beat a little faster when Roo's name popped up on the screen. We'd grown closer in recent months and I harboured a secret hope that our friendship would eventually become a romance.

I was pleased to see a message from him. But it wasn't our usual stream of warm banter. It read something to the effect of: 'I think God is really doing something in you. I don't want to get in the way of that so I think we should put "us" to one side for now.'

It was interesting. The message was an admission of where we had been heading, which was very nice to hear. But there was also a red stoplight and that hurt a little. For a moment my heart fell. But instead of hitting the floor and shattering like the brittle thing it was, it seemed to bounce up and land right back in my chest. It was as if it was attached to some

Hallmark springy gift-tag. It stayed put, bouncing gently, surrounded by a warm pink light.

The memory of the night before at church came flooding into my spirit, and I felt comfort and intrigue. As I hopped into the shower those words, 'Jesus cares – he cares for you' flashed up in my head like some gooey text message from a long-lost love. Have you ever loved someone from afar? There's chemistry and flirting but never an admission of feelings? It felt as if I'd just found out that Jesus was interested in me. Far from feeling like something had just ended, I felt that something amazing had just begun.

As I continued to get ready I began looking for a Bible. I was intrigued to hear more of what Jesus had to say. I fished through my bottom drawer and there beneath Year 8 artwork and piles of schoolbooks was that 'little red book': a New Testament that all students were given in Year 7. I'd written my name on the front sleeve. I threw it into my bag and headed for the bus stop.

For the first time in years the bus was on time. I hopped on and settled in for the long journey to Barnsley. My parent's place is out in the sticks, so public transport has never been a joy. But on this occasion it provided a great chance to road-test this mysterious book.

THE LITTLE RED BOOK

IGATHERED with the other applicants at the Alhambra offices, waiting to be interviewed. Despite being desperate for some quick cash, I felt relaxed. I remember giving a pep talk to one of the girls (despite her being my elf competition) and helping her relax before her interview.

A charming girl named Kate interviewed me. We even had a few giggles. Before I left, Kate told me I had one of the positions. I was over the moon. Despite the day starting off a little strangely, I felt things were taking an upward turn.

I went on from Barnsley to my sister Alex's house in Huddersfield. Alex had always been a rock to me. Nine years my senior, I was just a snotty kid when she entered her turbulent teen years. We'd been extra close since my teens. During tough times I used to escape to her place. She lived alone with her young daughter at the time and it was a warm, cosy environment in which to seek refuge. After my messy break-up, I'd turned to Alex again and our cosy chats over a cigarette always helped me to put things in perspective. She'd always been open to my spiritual musings and seen me collect a library of books on New Age ideas and practices.

The bus journey to her house was another long one. The bus wound through hills and dales as far as the eye could see. The only sign of civilization at one point was the TV mast that stood proudly against the Yorkshire evening sky.

I settled myself at the back of the bus. I had a new job and a sense of freedom I'd not felt in a while. Partly through boredom and partly through intrigue, I decided to get out the little red book again. I began to read. As I poured over the miniature pages I found myself absorbed. I started to read about Jesus and his life. The layout was user-friendly and it was a good place to start reading the Bible.

I discovered Paul's letters. They had a conversational quality about them as if they were speaking into my own life, just like the Roberta Flack song 'Killing Me Softly'. It made me feel a little embarrassed and flushed because it was so personal to me.

As I continued to read, it was as though a veil had been lifted from my vision and for the first time I could understand this stuff. It was clicking into place. This Jesus person was becoming easier to understand.

BANG BANG! A hoody-clad youth rapped on the window beside me as he left the bus. I almost lifted a foot off the orange seat. My heart was pounding. I had been so relaxed a moment ago, caught up in the deep reading experience, and suddenly I was totally on edge as though some force wanted to distract me.

I was still on edge when I reached Alex's house, but cup of tea in hand quickly relaxed into catch-up mode. I told her about my church experience. I told her that I was starting to think there was really something in this 'Jesus stuff'. I felt different. She was interested and very pleased about the job too. Then I told her about the text message from Roo. She knew how close we'd become.

'It's weird,' I said. 'I feel . . . fine. It's weird, I just feel like I have a new beginning in front of me and I'm totally fine about being single.'

I think even Alex was impressed by this revelation. But it was true. I felt at peace.

CHANGING CHANNELS

THAT NIGHT, I stayed up late at Alex's. She was working and studying at university and had to be up at the crack of dawn to get my baby niece, Lucy, ready for playgroup. I stayed downstairs while she went up to bed. I flicked through the cable channels looking for something to watch. Some late-night movie was playing and I settled on it for a time. A few minutes in, the inevitable sex scene unfolded. I had always been quite relaxed about such things. I was an open-minded twenty-first-century teen, but something felt different tonight.

The scene, which was quite graphic, made me feel uneasy. It wasn't that I thought it was immoral; I just didn't like the way it made me feel. It felt like the cheapening of something valuable. It made me a little sad to see a beautiful girl taking off her clothes for anyone and everyone to see. It made me feel angry to see a man becoming nothing more than an animal ruled by his hormones.

I began to think about Paul's letters again. I curiously pulled the red book from my handbag, wondering if I'd find some explanation for this sudden disquiet in my senses.

A shift was happening in the way I perceived things. It was as though the lens through which I'd been squinting at the world was clearing. I'd always imagined that sex was something Christianity was concealing from Christians. For the first time, my mind opened to the possibility that perhaps God just had better intentions for it.

TBC

AS THE WEEK progressed I found myself struggling with the 'God stuff' a little. It was consuming my thoughts. I was addicted to the little red New Testament. As I read the Bible it began to scare me. I read about Jesus and how his death had set me free from sin. But as I began to think about 'sin' I started to feel condemnation. According to God's standards, I'd been way off the scale. And I felt like a complete novice – a baby again. I was embarking on a journey into the unknown.

I also started to worry about how all of this was going to affect my life. Who was the new Philippa going to be? The strangest part was that I felt I'd started something that wasn't going to stop. It was as if I'd rubbed the magic lamp and the genie wasn't going back in in a hurry.

I had arranged to go to an event that Saturday with Andy Baker and Roo. Andy was sure it was something I should go to. It was a Christmas ball being thrown by a Christian media company. He assured me there was a bar and I fully intended to use it. I was interested to see what these 'Christian pop stars' had to offer. I'd never really come across any Christian music that I thought was any good.

I was excited to see Roo. I couldn't wait to update him on my experiences that week. He was going to be very surprised. After months of encouraging me to go further with Jesus, I'd crossed the line and something was definitely happening.

We arrived at the ball dressed in a bit of a silly way. It was supposed to be a 'Bad-taste Ball', which was OK until the first act came out dressed like pop stars. A band called TBC burst onto the stage and went right into an energetic dance routine. The lead singer, Shell, led the band with a warm confidence and distinctive vocals. She was a girl-next-door type with irresistible charm and unnerving self-assurance.

The girls were stunning and blew the audience away with their stage presence. I'd always been confident about one thing – my value as a performer – but this was on a different level. The real phenomenon was that they were singing about a relationship with God.

I still felt the band was representing a club I couldn't be part of. I felt like a freak in comparison. I met the girls afterwards and they seemed fairly normal. Andy, Roo and I went for a drink in the bar. I hit the lager. I was so self-conscious that I'd be seen drinking and looked around frantically to find 'one of them' holding a pint or a glass of wine. I only clocked one and downed my drink nervously before anyone could see.

I told Andy and Roo about my week. They were amazed.

'Wow, something's definitely happening,' Roo said.

'Seriously,' I said, 'there's no turning back.' It was like I'd drunk some sort of potion and was transforming whether I liked it or not.

On the drive home we talked about TBC. 'I should write them some songs. I bet I could write great Christian pop songs.'

Andy started to bring me down a peg.

'It doesn't really work like that,' he said.

'I can write songs about Jesus,' I defended. 'It's easy.' I felt Andy was suggesting I wasn't capable, or worse still, not worthy.

'It's not as easy as that. You have to know Scripture. You have to spend time making sure the lyrics are appropriate.'

'Why can't I just write from my heart? Just because I haven't always been a Christian doesn't mean I can't write a song about it.' The atmosphere was strained. Andy knew he'd upset me.

'Anyway, I'm thinking of applying to be in one of those bands.' The MC had made an announcement during the evening that Innovation was looking for new talent to serve in their schools' band.

'I could do that,' I said.

'Philippa, you've been a Christian for ten minutes, and that might not be the right direction for you. Some of those girls have worked for years on no salary to get to that position.' Now I was totally offended.

'I'm just so fed up trying to work out what my life's all about!' Hot tears pricked the whites of my eyes. Something was definitely shifting in me. I could tell that whatever this process was it wasn't going to be easy. Growth is bound to cause some growing pains.

Andy could see I was struggling and tried to encourage me. I couldn't hear by this point. In the end Andy offered to take me to another church the following day. It was the church he belonged to when he was at uni.

Out with the Old

I HAD HEARD incredible things about 'The Anvil'. It was a youth service held in an impressive large church in Ecclesall, an affluent part of Sheffield. It's a place with beautiful houses and clever children. Families go climbing and picnicking in the Peak District. People paint their own pictures for the hallway and bake their own bread.

I felt nervous as I walked into the impressive church: a breath-taking building filled with a lively, mixed bag of teenagers and young adults. Bubbly Beth greeted me as I walked nervously into the narthex.

She introduced herself and offered immediate support. It was clear I was being treated as a special guest with great respect and care. There was the ever-present enthusiasm I'd seen in all Christians (they were keen for you to become a part of their crew). They even had youth-group merchandise. And very cool it was too – re-styled Bibles, branded pens, journals and badges, all impeccably designed with striking graphics.

Once inside, their 'time of worship' began, but it was quite unlike anything I'd ever seen or imagined. They were worshipping to a CD. There were over 100 teenagers singing their hearts out.

After the music had finished we sat down to hear the 'message'. It became obvious at this point what the branded pens and note-pads were for. The teenagers scribbled away, hanging on the speaker's every word. The speaker in this case was Andrew Seaton – a studious-looking, confident guy in his late twenties with designer spectacles.

As he began to speak, I felt my skin prickle. He was talking about getting rid of the old you and putting on a new you. He used a visual aid of a jacket – off came the old jacket, dirty and worn, yet comfortable. On went the new jacket, clean and sparkly, yet not so snug and comfortable.

I felt uncomfortable. I understood the message but hated the idea of getting rid of the old me. I hated the idea of having to totally change. I left the meeting feeling a deeper sense of confusion than before.

It was both the best and the worst I had ever felt.

Words Come to Life

THE FOLLOWING DAY, I was still in knots. The speaker's words kept ringing in my mind: 'You have to take off the old, comfortable you and put on the new, clean you.' It sounded so intense. I wasn't sure if I could subscribe to this. I thought about those teenagers, totally sold out to this cause. Their lives were all about one thing, or should I say, one person: Jesus.

I called Roo in a panic.

'Hey how are you?' he answered, cheerful as usual.

'Not good really,' I admitted. 'I went to The Anvil last night and I hated it.'

'Really?' he said. 'Why?'

'I don't know, I just thought that the speaker seemed really judgmental. I've come away feeling terrified of this God stuff.' Roo, being a relatively new, but far more established Christian than I, referred to the things he'd heard at church.

'I think that's a good thing isn't it? I think the Bible says, "The fear of the Lord is the beginning of wisdom."' I hated his answer; I hated the idea of embracing any kind of fear. It was too close to home.

'No Roo, it's not good. It's terrible! I've lived in fear all my life. Part of the reason I asked God for help is that I didn't want to live in fear anymore. You can't tell me now that my destiny is to live in fear for the rest of my life.' Roo wasn't going to argue this with me.

'Yeah, I don't know then. Man, I'm really angry with the guys from The Anvil. You were doing so well!'

'I know,' I said. 'Anyway, I guess I'll see you on your birthday.' We hung up and I did the only thing I could think of to do, I reluctantly went back to the little red book that had been causing 'the problem'.

I opened it and my heart started to beat faster as I read. Under the heading 'Suffering for being a Christian' it said:

> Dear friends, do not be surprised at the painful trial you are suffering, as though something strange were happening to you. But rejoice that you participate in the sufferings of Christ, so that you may be overjoyed when his glory is revealed (1 Peter 4:12–13).

At this I was completely freaked out, ever more convinced that God was doing something in my life. I had asked for him to show up and it seemed . . . he had.

CONQUERING DEMONS

I HAD relied on cigarettes to manage stress since my early teens. I had tried to quit countless times. If you're a smoker you'll know it's no easy task. There was always an excuse to keep smoking – the stress of a break-up, exams or celebrating exam results. Every smoker knows that having a glass of wine or a beer makes for instant smokers' weakness.

In the back of my mind I had every intention of quitting. As an aspiring singer it was a barrier for improvement, and there's nothing worse than the looming idea that you're damaging your health. I knew that cigarettes were just another dangerous crutch. Smoking was making me less than I ought to be. So, when I began to feel like my life was changing it seemed like the right time to kick the habit.

Just a week after I'd asked Jesus to come into my life, something tragic happened. One of my sister's close friends took his own life after years of struggling with addiction. It was devastating and depressing. I was glad that I'd found faith. At least I could believe that Jesus may have been with him in his final hours.

My sister took me along to the funeral. There's no joy at a funeral where someone has taken his own life. That week I had resolved to quit smoking and the funeral was day two of giving up. I made it through the day despite everyone offering me smokes and there being a lot of therapeutic drinking going on.

Afterwards, we made our way back to Alex's house and stood in her kitchen. It was a regular smoking location for us, away from where my niece Lucy played. Alex cranked the windows wide open and lit a cigarette. After a moment she heard Lucy crying from the upstairs bedroom. Rushing to comfort her daughter, she left the burning cigarette in the ashtray.

I stared at it. It was right there. Just me and the cigarette. Maybe I could just have a drag? I'd done so well after all; no one would even know. The temptation was subtle but intense. It was just a cigarette after all, but it also represented a massive threat to my voice, my health and my self-control. At that moment, I felt the presence of strong conviction in my heart – a gentle sober voice: 'If you can resist that "one drag" you'll have conquered this. If you can make it through this moment without smoking you can make it through any moment.'

I walked over to the sink, poured a glass of water and squared up. I resisted. Since that day, I have never picked up a cigarette again. With the spirit of truth battling through me I was able to make a change that I'd never had the strength to before. At the worst possible time I found the strength to overcome temptation.

From House to Home

FOR OBVIOUS REASONS, a cloud hung over the weeks that followed. It wasn't just the pain of losing someone I'd known, there's a heavy smoke that lingers around a death of that nature. It's such a waste of life.

I was clinging onto the words of comfort in my little Bible. Pouring over it thirstily. I felt a little lost without the cigarettes. I was over the worst for sure, but giving up was yet another thing in my life that had changed.

Roo and I had remained friends and still met up to rehearse for shows and to work on new material. We'd been working with the guys from the dance label on club tracks, but were gently evolving into an acoustic act.

Now it seemed that my connection with this record label was withering too. For a time the record label had been the most important thing I had going. Throughout the previous summer I had been visiting Inspirit Records at least once a week (a habit my credit card bills reflected). It gave me a reason to get out of bed in the morning.

But after being repeatedly put on the back burner I had a bit of a falling out with the label manager. I was bitterly disappointed. The ground felt anything but safe.

But in a strange way, I was opening up musically. After moving back home I fell in love with my dad's acoustic guitar. Dad had shown me a couple of chords years earlier, but I'd never quite mastered them. Now, with the extra time on my hands I was finally getting to grips with the basics. In the still of the night while my parents slept I picked up the guitar and picked out chords I didn't know the names of.

Warm December Chill

I CONTINUED my job as a Christmas Elf. It was easy work with some amusing perks. The portrait photos of kids with Santa were 90 per cent crying shots. It was a real Christmas eye-opener.

At the same time my relationship with Roo was slowly turning into something more. We had a connection. We were friends and partners in music. But he'd taken an even greater position in my life by being central to my 'transformation' process. Don't get me wrong – Roo wasn't like a mentor. He was a flame that drew me to faith. Such was my admiration for him that I'd follow wherever he wanted to go. In the car one day somewhere between Preston and Sheffield he asked me to be his girlfriend and I accepted.

I began to feel that God was leading me through the fog. For the first time at Christmas, I felt like I was closer to the birthday boy. There was still a lot of work to do in me and in my life, but for the first time in years there was real hope.

This kind of thing has happened on several occasions in my life. It was as though someone had turned up the colours in my world after a grey spell. Things look bleak and suddenly light seeps though. This usually happened to me when summer arrived. But this time I knew it was different – it was in the dark night of winter.

Standing in my room one night, I placed a small picture postcard of Jesus on my dresser, moving the dragons and fairies to a box below. I stuck on a CD Andy had given me some time earlier. It read on the front: *Hillsong and Delirious? Live* above a picture of a packed auditorium.

The music began. I skipped track one. Then as track two swelled I heard the most heavenly voice. It was clear and supple and pure. It reminded me of voices I'd studied and adored in my teens, but this voice had an added layer of something special. The singer's name was Darlene.

As I listened to her sing of her desire to honour and worship God, the warmest, dizziest feeling came upon me. It was almost involuntary, but so welcome. It was the same feeling I'd had the morning I had that text message from Roo. It was a peace that I'd never felt in all my life. It surpassed understanding.

The transitions continued through Christmas and into the New Year. By this time Roo and I were dating and it was just coming up to my twenty-first birthday. Guitar was becoming easier and I'd even started to write a couple of new songs.

I'd visited the Freedom Centre Church several times by now. It was a great place. It was a sapling church that didn't have its own building. Instead, they met in a line-dancing hall. The first time I went in I more or less kept myself to myself, not wanting to stand out as the 'beginner' Christian. I sang along quietly. Roo's friend Pete (who'd prayed for me in halls) asked how I was doing with my journey.

'Not too bad,' I said. 'I'm still figuring things out to be honest.'

'Don't worry, just take your time.' They always welcomed me patiently. It amazed me how willing people were to let

God into their lives. The girls were beautiful. There was nothing nerdy or religious about them. But when they prayed and sang they became overwhelmed by God's presence.

It was surreal seeing tea and coffee being served over a bar. The service was led from a stage surrounded by old barrels and bales of hay. I'll never forget the first time I went to the church. The air vents let in shards of light that fell into the congregation. They seemed to come as soon as we started singing. After spending my teens sleeping in until noon every Sunday, getting out of bed to sing with the sun on my face felt like another life. I visited the church on the weekends I was visiting Roo.

I'd also been attending The Anvil in Sheffield on Sunday nights. The people there were amazing. The pastor of this radical youth movement was a guy called Andy Rushworth. He was completely the opposite of anything you'd picture at the mention of a minister. He was in his forties with a young family and gorgeous wife, Sharon. He had the presence of someone who could take the world on. He was a tall, strong guy with a shaved head and two full sleeves of body art. Each tattoo was a work of art that glorified God in some way.

He made me realize that there was a reason to be a Christian. It wasn't just about having a better life – there was more. We live in a generation that needs radical change. Young people are lost and looking for meaning in all the wrong places. I could deeply relate to this.

I also made a lifelong friend in Steph Cook. She had grown up in a Christian family. Her parents were bona fide do-gooders. Del, Steph's mum, was well known for her lifestyle of evangelism. She spent her free time taking food to the needy in her neighbourhood.

Steph found her own way with faith in her late teens after a rebellious spell. We hit it off straight away. She had the most infectious laugh and a huge heart. She helped me to feel like I'd come home. For the first time in months I felt I belonged.

I was facing a tough decision though. With the pressure at home, and a growing need to spread my wings and do something with my life, I was looking to move out of home. I'd loved Preston. It had the Freedom Centre and Roo. But I also loved Sheffield and it was closer to home. It was a tough decision. I wasn't sure what career opportunities Sheffield would present. It certainly wasn't the best place to look for any kind of record deal. The decision was playing on my mind.

Worship

ONE SUNDAY NIGHT we were at The Anvil. Andy Rushworth turned up before the service started.

'You wanna get her singing in the worship tonight,' Andy said to a member of the team. I couldn't believe it! I'd thought about singing in church the first moment I set foot in there, but I had no idea when I might be ready to do that. I was so nervous.

'What worship songs do you know?' Andy asked.

'Erm, I don't know . . . Oh there is one that I really like. It's on a Hillsong CD. I don't have the lyrics though.'

'We can get 'em. Sing it to Sean.' I sang a little of the melody to the guitarist and he recognized the song.

'There you go, John will print 'em out in the office for you.'

And that was it. I was singing.

I found Steph before the service started and told her how nervous I was.

'I'm so scared I'm not ready for this. I've never sung in church before,' I shared.

'You'll be absolutely fine. I really think God will use you.' Steph prayed for me and the service started. At the right moment during the meeting, they invited me to sing.

I began to sing and my voice bounced around the huge building. I shut my eyes tight and tried to focus on nothing but God. I wasn't even used to playing with a band. All my life I'd only performed with my dad, Roo or over tracks. The band followed the flow of the song and for the first time I experienced singing in worship. I opened my eyes a little and noticed everyone was focusing on not me but on *God*. Steph was standing right in the middle of the aisle with her eyes shut and her arms outstretched. It was an amazing feeling of belonging to a bigger purpose.

When the meeting closed Andy came to congratulate me on my first song in church. I felt like something special had taken place in me. I loved the feeling of going to another level through music. It did something to my voice that I'd never experienced before. I was impressed by Andy's willingness to take a gamble on me. After much thought and prayer I decided that I should try to move to Sheffield.

I thought that this was the right group of people to be around. It confused Roo, but for some reason Preston just didn't feel like the right place – even though I was so fond of him.

It's hard to explain how exactly I knew, but Sheffield was where the next chapter of life would take place. I told my parents and they were very supportive. They were a little concerned about my music career. But I explained that I needed to make a life for myself. When it came to music I had no idea what would become of me. But I knew that my faith had opened up a new dimension in my creativity. I was playing guitar more and writing songs.

Around that time I wrote a song called 'Crazy Days'. It was a tribute to my former self and a thank you to 'the man upstairs' for preserving me. When I played it to Roo and Andy they were excited to hear me playing guitar and singing.

There was an interesting mix of influences – all of my favourite music with faith-inspired lyrics.

Family

WEEK BY WEEK my heart was igniting. I would listen to Andy Rushworth speaking from the heart about purpose and passion. During one meeting he began speaking about how we were called 'for such a time as this'. As a new Christian it resonated. I began to see how I might fit into the bigger picture.

By this time my folks were beginning to raise their eyebrows at my newfound faith. They liked Roo and they'd met Andy once or twice. They both knew the past six months had taken me close to the edge. It seemed that this 'faith' business had come along at the right time. But they were equally aware of my vulnerability. There were a couple of family occasions that I opted out of much to everyone's concern (I love BBQs, and to choose church over Mum's soy pork was enough to worry anyone).

My folks only knew the rebel Philippa – lethargic and troubled. They only knew Philippa who lived at her boyfriend's house and came back for food and clean clothes. They weren't used to an upbeat and optimistic daughter, so it got their attention. Any good parent would question such a change. Of course, this was tough for me at the time. I felt like I couldn't win. I'd gone from being a skinny chain-smoker engulfed in doom to a bright, effervescent Jesus lover. It wasn't the ideal swap, but I thought it was an obvious step forward.

One night, we erupted into argument. I was reading Dad something from the New Testament, plucking out an excerpt like one might reel off a headline over breakfast, 'Government passes anti-cloning bill'. Except it was more like, 'Whoever calls upon the name of the Lord will be saved'.

It seemed to be a by-product of being 'born-again' – a rainbow-bright zeal for faith that came with no filter. I was keen to share what was happening to me. I felt like an ugly duckling that kept waking up every morning covered in a new layer of neon feathers.

For the first time in my life, I felt Dad wasn't 100 per cent behind me. He wasn't going to fight my corner on this. That night some harsh words were exchanged. He told me he didn't believe and that he could never believe. He said he disapproved of my faith. I was overcome with frustration.

Through hot tears I vented an explosion of internal insecurity, 'Really? You preferred things before did you, when I was in a total mess? I wanted to die!' I slipped off to my room. Flopping onto the edge of the bed I began to sob. In the heavy silence I looked around the room. The room had been recently decorated. My connection with it felt as shallow as that with my new self.

I looked at the growing collection of Jesus postcards across the bottom of my mirror, souvenirs picked up from the Christian bookshop. One was a print of Holman Hunt's famous painting 'Jesus – Light of the World', which shows Jesus at a door with a softly glowing lantern. There were also a couple of slightly dodgy remnants from my New Age phase: a dream-catcher someone made me as a gift, a book about shamanic medicine and an odd dragon statue sat about my dresser like gargoyles on an old university building.

The evening sun was drifting lower as the evening loomed. The window of my childhood room looks out onto a disused road, then our garden and eventually a large woodland that separates us from the motorway. Ah, the motorway – the gentle hum that mingled with birdsong and cricket chorus for as a long as I can remember. The light bubbled in, hitting my decorative mirror-ball and landing in silver flecks all over the walls. I stared into space, reaching for the inner voice, trying to hear the guidance of God through the quarrel within.

I found myself humming, the shapes of words forming on my lips, 'Home is not where the broken heart is. It's not somewhere you feel you are alone.'

It no longer mattered where I lived, or whom I was with. I had a place somewhere, with God.

THE PRAYER CARD

I'M A CHILD of the eighties so I vividly remember the emerging of the Magic Eye Picture phenomenon. For any of you that missed it, in the early nineties some clever IT genius figured out how to imbed images within seemingly formless patterns. On the face of it they were merely gaudy coloured patterns, but if you were to study them long enough, and with a slight refocusing of your eyes you would begin to find the hidden picture.

The first time it happened I was so relieved. I was in on the secret. I had learned the formula. What was once a bunch of lines and swirls was a huge shark's mouth, jutting out of the picture with sharp teeth and bulging eyes. In many ways, that's what my first visit to the Freedom Centre after asking Jesus to reveal himself to me was like.

What was once a bunch of enthusiastic, squeaky-clean, slightly barmy people was now a room filled with praising saints. The atmosphere was tangible. The music seemed to have different dimensions to it. As I sang and focused on lyrics filled with reverence, passion and truth, my soul seemed to move in time.

The songs were deep and therapeutic. It was in these times of worship that I learned to offload my issues. The lyrics were loaded with Scripture and encouragement to sooth my soul. And as the room lifted its song, I'd close my eyes and allow those united voices filled with the deepest songs of their hearts to wash over me and through me. I would walk into these meetings heavy, and come out lighter. I would walk in with years of negative thought patterns engulfing my mind and walk out liberated, filled instead with positive thoughts.

After the meeting, Pete came over. He was a tall, lean and gentle twenty-something, the embodiment of what a youth worker should be. He was ever so slightly Narnia-like with a wisp of facial hair and quizzical eyes. His clothes were always relevant and, despite anything you might find to question or criticize about him, he was someone who always made you feel safe. Like one trained in 'being nice to people'. I often felt I wanted to test his limits just to see. I wondered if all transactions were being monitored for training and quality purposes. But truth be known, you'd hope and pray that if you cut him in half you'd see the same substance right through his middle. He was pure good. Everything down to his accent was youth worker-like. He was always a total gentleman.

This particular morning I was looking forward to catching up with him. We hadn't really spoken since my 'conversion'. He came over to chat, visibly surprised to see me so engrossed in the worship.

'Hey Philippa, how are you doing? It's great to see you here.' We chatted briefly before Roo bounced over and we all began filtering out of the line-dancing hall. That day was a landmark occasion for the small church. Pastor Jack had explained during the meeting that Tesco had amazingly agreed to allow the church to meet in one of their office blocks on the docks. Tesco was loaning them the building rent-free.

After the meeting the group went to check out the proposed new location. Roo bounced through each room excitedly as the pastor's wife Sue painted imaginary pictures of how each room would function.

'And here we'll have the prayer room. Such and such is working on a life-sized cross for us and we have Charlene working on some prophetic art for us too. We'll be able to pray over the whole city,' she explained excitedly.

Roo was visibly enthused too. At that time, church seemed to be the most important thing in his world. Sometimes I found it hard to compete. Part of me still felt like damaged goods and that I wasn't as good as the other Christians there. I felt sure I'd say the wrong thing or make some huge faith faux pas in public.

Once on the top floor of the building the group began to disburse, exploring small rooms and riffling through the empty cupboards.

Pete, Roo, Library Matt and I parked in the space at the edge of the room beneath the slanted attic window. Staring out at the Preston Docks we began chatting about my past few weeks.

'I just feel totally different. I find myself reading the Bible and it's like the words just grab me. It's as if the world is changing!'

Pete smiled, his bright youth worker eyes glittering in the afternoon light. He laughed as I reeled off my little run of 'coincidences' in the past weeks. With a wry, sideways grin he said, 'I didn't know what to think when I saw you singing and jumping around at church this morning. I was like, "Is this for real?" I mean, no offence, but after those conversations we had at the flat, I thought you were a long way off believing. You were quite hard work.'

I was surprised to hear him say that. I know I gave them a hard time. But I thought that was the natural thing for a non-believer to do. He continued, 'But speaking to you now it's obvious that God's massively at work in your life!' I grinned in agreement. 'It's a really amazing answer to prayer.'

'Really?' I said, flattered. Then he showed me.

'We've had a prayer card season.' He leafed through his well-worn Bible, the cover hanging off like it had narrowly escaped a shredder attack. From between the dog-eared pages he produced a strip of pale blue card. It had a printed border topped by the Freedom Centre logo. On it was a list of names. Somewhere down the list was my name, spelled completely wrong. I was touched to think, this whole time, someone had been hoping I'd turn a corner. A stranger had seen something good in me.

'It's amazing because quite a few people have been praying for you,' he added.

'Really? No way! Who?'

'Well,' he said eyeing Roo cheekily, 'Roo I would hope.' Roo cast me a look.

'Yes, I have been praying for you a lot.' Pete grinned at Roo.

'And Saphirra has been praying for you as well I think.' Hearing her name, a bubbly girl in her late teens with exotic eyes and great accessories came to join us. She confirmed with great enthusiasm that she too had put me on the prayer list. I couldn't believe it!

I loved the Freedom Centre. There was such vitality about it. Jack and Sue were very Holy Spirit-centred. They wanted to operate 'in the spirit' at all times. They prayed constantly about ways they might reach the people of Preston. It was a real journey for me. I became passionate about prayer and its power.

One afternoon while Roo was sick in bed with tonsillitis I went to the church alone. I was helping them prepare for the first Sunday in the new building. Sue was making curtains and tablecloths. People were stacking board games away in the kiddies' room and stocking cupboards with enough tea and biscuits to sink a battle ship. Everyone on the team was full of life and excitement – and many of them were my age or younger.

I was intent on making sure that my new faith was authentic. I was a bit confused up to this point.

Pete had said, 'I always saw you as a Freedom Centre person.' I wasn't sure if I shared his vision. There was so much I loved about being there. I loved going there with Roo. Sometimes I wondered if I was just latching onto his passion instead of having my own. Especially since in the complicated exchanges of my recent break-up, that suggestion had been made several times.

For the time being, we went to both the Freedom Centre and The Anvil. I started to look forward to the weekends like never before. Sunday used to be a dull and dread-filled day, anticipating school or work the following day. Sundays were now the highlight and the lifeline of my week.

Special Gifts

THE NIGHTS drew in. I made regular trips to the city on a hill (as Preston is known). I attended socials and prayer meetings.

Andy Baker was at university in Preston so he was often there. He lived with Jack and Sue for a spell. Their house was a magical converted barn.

Christmas was beautiful. The fog in my head had lifted. I'd spent some time with Roo and his family and they were great to be around (not to mention Roo's mum's amazing onion sauce). I'll never forget playing the cardboard box game. The whole family has to stand in a circle and one by one pick up the box from the floor using only their teeth. When each person had completed the task an inch would be cut from the box to make it harder. If you fall over you're out. Roo's elderly grandpa almost beat me once, very embarrassing.

After we'd had Sunday dinner one day we got in the car to head back to Sheffield. Roo reached into the glove box and pulled out some gifts. I was confused; we'd already swapped gifts days ago.

'They're not from me, they're from an old friend of yours.' I was a little nervous as I pulled off the shiny paper. But there it was – a Bible.

All of this time I'd been using the little red New Testament from school. But I had noticed that others were carrying round the whole Bible. I asked Andy Baker about the Old Testament. I had assumed it wasn't all that important since Jesus changed everything anyway. He explained that Jesus wasn't just a New Testament afterthought, but actually had been prophetically involved in the whole story right from Genesis, and referred to by all of the prophets.

'Wow,' I said. I didn't expect that. We drove to Yorkshire and to the evening service at The Anvil. Andy came over to greet us.

'Hey Philippa, I've got you a present,' he said. Out came the second unexpected gift of the day. This one was slightly bigger. You guessed it. It was a Bible. I loved it. It was purple with a concordance. Steph bounced up behind me to give me a hug.

'It's the same as mine!' she said.

In with the New

I RETURNED to The Anvil after Christmas Day. It was so odd, the negative feeling I'd had from my first trip had gone. I had realized that getting to know God wasn't like joining a religion where I'd never be able to live up to expectations. I was realizing that God had always been a part of my life. He'd always had a plan for me and it was more like coming home.

I decided from the start that I would always go to God with my questions as well as to other Christians. It was wise to ask advice from people you trust. But whatever you hear about God, the way you should live, or God's opinion of you, you should always see what Scripture has to say about it too.

I wrote in my diary one night:

I feel it's important to listen to God with your own ears. If the great prophets of our time had only listened to each other we'd never have heard the message. I've been reading the Word. Then I stare into the sky and see the beauty of the universe. I believe the Word because I see its resonance in nature and in true love. Then little by little the shell of my ego and my self-importance is shaken brittle by the presence of the Spirit within. It starts to flake away! I feel like I'm growing down! Releasing my bitterness and hardness from anger and pain and confusion to reveal a new skin. And I can't help but notice that my heart feels clean. And the questioning that terrified me and stopped me believing,

the part that's always stopped me from being my best self, starts to lose
its power as I absorb . . . the truth. I no longer look for contradictions
in the Bible and in Christians, and I start to search for understanding.

As I read back this entry I can see what was happening. First, I was reconciling this Bible with the things I already understood about myself and about life. I had to find where it would fit with me. Also, I was changing, and I could feel it. After asking for God to come into my life I came across a passage in the New Testament. It said, '. . . because our gospel came to you not simply with words but also with power, with the Holy Spirit and deep conviction' (1 Thessalonians 1:5).

It was more than just words that were having an effect on my life. The Bible claimed that when you ask Jesus into your life you become filled with the Holy Spirit. Jesus himself comes into your heart and begins to change you.

And wherever Jesus is, miracles happen.

Alpha

THERE WAS still much I needed to understand about faith. I had so many unanswered questions. I was confused about issues such as life after death. Was there really a heaven and a hell? Was there really such a thing as the devil? I really struggled with this one. It just seemed too far-fetched and to be honest, too dark to entertain.

My mum has always had an interest in Jesus. I recall when we were younger she would always talk about him when Christmas or Easter came around. She was always keen to embrace the meaning behind the holiday. I had no problem with this. But when I was asked to accompany my mum to an Alpha Course aged sixteen, my response was suitably dismissive.

'No way, man. I'm not interested in that. I have better things to do.'

So Mum observed the changes in me as a result of my new-found faith with a keen interest. When I told her that I'd asked God to take over my life and that I believed things were actually happening, it ignited a new spark in her to seek God too. My sister was also intrigued after hearing about my experiences, and took the liberty of signing all three of us up for Alpha at a church near her house.

A chap called Nicky Gumbel, a barrister who decided to become a Vicar after an encounter with God, developed the

Alpha course. The result was a very clever communication of the case for faith.

The course involved going to a local church, having a free meal (donations welcome), watching a short 'talk' by Nicky Gumbel on DVD and then discussing it in groups.

Each week he would cover a different FAQ about Christianity. The magical thing was, this whole process was happening without me even understanding the mechanics of it. But I was keen to learn more about Jesus.

I agreed to go along. My sister wasn't keen on it after the first couple of times. But Mum and I stuck with it. We quickly found that the course seemed to be addressing our concerns with spooky accuracy.

My dad is a gifted and talented performer. I learned to love music and to use my voice by listening to Dad and watching him on stage. He had always been my hero. I was always a daddy's girl. There's a picture of me on holiday aged six wearing a cap with 'I love my daddy' on it. I distinctly remember choosing that cap from a pile of 'I love [insert family member]' hats. He was my world.

But the dynamic in our family began to change when Mum and I started Alpha. It was obvious that something was happening. God seemed to be drawing us close for the first time in years and Dad felt strange about the whole thing. He was raised in the Irish Catholic tradition and had never felt faith. He had never seen anything in the church that suggested God was good, or even real. So when I told him I'd become a Christian I may as well have said I was joining the circus. He said he'd never believe.

One day while I was reading the Bible I became filled with a terrifying thought. What if my dad wasn't going to heaven?

I couldn't stomach the idea of him not being there with me. My Christian teaching was telling me that in order to be with God after you leave the world, you have to ask Jesus into your heart and believe! Dad was saying he would never believe that. I just couldn't come to terms with it.

I sat in our office at home and cried out to God, tears streaming down my face.

'I can't believe that you'd send my dad to hell! I just can't cope with it. If that's the case then I can't believe in you because I don't believe God would send someone like my dad to hell. Please help me understand, because I can't go on like this,' I cried out.

It was a desperate moment. I couldn't continue as a Christian with this question on my mind. But also, there seemed to be no going back, which left me in a state of limbo.

I opened my Bible desperately hoping for a word of encouragement. Written on the page in front of me was this verse: 'It is written: "'As surely as I live,' says the Lord, 'Every knee will bow before me; every tongue will confess to God'"' (Romans 14:11).

I thought about it. This certainly seemed to be a response to my questions. But this was serious stuff. How could I be sure that reading the verse wasn't just a coincidence? And did this really mean that my dad was going to find God? Or did it mean that God would have his opportunity to invite everyone to heaven regardless of when they might die?

'God please let this be true. Please help me have peace about this,' I prayed.

The following day, Mum and I went to the Alpha Course. We had a delicious meal and settled in the quaint old church building to watch the DVD. That week's topic was 'Why Did Jesus Die?'

'Interesting,' I thought to myself. I'd never really understood the exact reason for Jesus going to the cross. It seemed so complicated.

I couldn't believe what I was hearing as Nicky began to speak. I listened in amazement as he explained that each of us had fallen short of the design God had for our lives. We each make mistakes in the way we treat others and ourselves. He explained that Jesus was the Son of God, in essence, God poured into a man's body, who was sent to live a perfect life and to lay it down willingly in place of ours. He died so that we could receive him and be pardoned of the consequences we deserved. He explained that in God's love he had found a solution that would make a way for us to know our father again and for us to live on after death. But this didn't answer my question about Dad. It still didn't seem fair. Then, my jaw dropped as Nicky Gumbel told the following story.

Nicky had lost his father. He was married and a Christian at the time of his father's passing, but like mine, his dad hadn't been a Christian. He too had been struggling with the idea of his father not going to heaven. Exactly ten days after his death, he was reading the Bible and asked God to speak to him about his father because he was still worrying about him. Nicky was reading Romans and came across the verse, 'Everyone who calls on the name of the Lord will be saved' (Romans 10:13). He sensed at that moment that God was saying to him that the verse was for his father; that he had called on the name of the Lord and been saved. About five minutes later his wife, Pippa, came in and said, 'I have been reading a verse in Acts 2:21 and I think this verse is for your father. It says, "And everyone who calls on the name of the Lord will be saved."' It was quite extraordinary, because that verse only appears twice in the New Testament and God had spoken to both of them through the same words at the same time in different parts of the Bible.

After hearing this I was satisfied that whether I understood it or not, God had a plan for everyone. I understood that I should do my best to share the gospel, but that I would never understand the mystery of God's will. I should just trust, and have faith that God was good.

This Alpha miracle was one of many. It seemed God was sharing something with Mum and me each week. We hadn't seen eye-to-eye since the spirit of the teenager descended into my life aged thirteen. Now, after all the tantrums and slammed doors we were finally unifying again.

At the end of the course Mum had made up her mind. She too wanted to throw her old life into God's hands and pick up a new one. So, now there were two . . .

THE RAILCARD MIRACLE

FOR YEARS (since my teens began) I'd suffered with panic rage. I'd become so flaky at arranging my life that things constantly seemed to go wrong. I began to expect the worst. I'd reach into my bag for my purse, and before I'd even looked properly I'd be on the phone cancelling cards and ordering new ones. I was also super forgetful. I was used to finding I'd missed payments on store cards and losing phones, purses and clothing. It was something I really needed help with.

One day, I was preparing to visit Roo in Preston. As a result of paying back store cards and other debts money was a little tight. As I prepared to leave for my train journey, which for once I'd booked in advance using my railcard for discount, I realized to my horror that my railcard was not in my bag. I panicked, emptying my handbag onto my bedroom floor.

'No way, I can't believe this!' I said aloud. I started to feel tears forming as I riffled through coat pockets, jeans' pockets and suitcase side pockets to no avail. Just as I was about to turn the air blue with swear words I took a moment to catch my breath.

I thought about Jesus and his promise to give me peace.

'It can't be right,' I thought. 'I'm so knotted up with anxiety and anger. There must be a way to be calm even in moments like this.' I sat on my bed, ready to surrender, and reached for my Bible.

'I'm choosing something different today,' I thought. 'Instead of losing my head about this, I'm just going to take it to God.'

I closed my eyes, took a deep breath and opened my Bible. From between the thin pages my railcard slid out gently onto my lap. I picked it up, filled with joy and relief. Coincidence or not, it seemed clear to me; there was never any need to panic.

Once again I realized I could trust God.

Believing in Love

IWAS never the kid that dreamed of her wedding. I know it's unusual. Little girls drape tablecloths over their heads and waltz down make-believe aisles before pledging vows to giant soft toys. Not me. I was too busy pretending to be Whitney Houston. But something was downloaded (figuratively speaking) to me on Chris and Shan's big day.

I was singing. That was a challenge in itself. A wedding – the biggest day of this couple's life – and I had the responsibility of representing Christianity before a mass of their family and friends.

The guests filed in dressed in their best. Weddings must be a good dating opportunity I concluded; everyone was very well turned out. The groom waited expectantly facing the front and turning round at odd intervals. I summed him up judgmentally. I saw him as a life-long Christian with no baggage – a perfect human being with a perfect family. I retracted my thoughts, suddenly very aware that he might be weighing me up too.

And then she appeared. The congregation stood expectantly and turned towards the entrance with baited breath. Glorious. Shan was the first 'born-again Christian' bride I'd seen. Veiled in purity, she was beautiful, radiant and glowing. My heart flooded with a kind of love and envy combined. This was truly magical. There was something different about it. Chris and Shan were a true Christian couple. They hadn't been sleeping together and now they were joining their lives together for God's purposes. It was fascinating.

As we sang and watched them make their vows a strange feeling came over me: this was what weddings were supposed to be – electrifying displays of love and commitment and the start of a new family.

Years on I became good friends with Chris and Shan. We watched the wedding video in their front room with coffee, biscuits and banter. They told me their day hadn't in fact been perfect. It was hard to believe from where I had been standing that morning. But what I was seeing was not human perfection; it was a picture of perseverance – an aspiration for something better.

Their hearts had still held doubts and fears. Their families had been quite normal with the usual pre-wedding drama. I even learned that after the ceremony they'd visited Chris's terminally ill dad in hospital. It hadn't been perfect. But what had fascinated me was the purity and holiness of that occasion.

I had seen something beautiful. I began to dream as a little girl might dream of her big day.

Coming of Age

I'LL NEVER FORGET my twenty-first birthday. I went out with friends and family for an intimate dinner. My folks and sister Alex were there along with close friends, and of course Roo.

At dinner I gave a toast, 'I just want to say thank you so much for coming tonight. I'm so blessed to have you in my life. I can honestly say my favourite people in the world are around this table! I'm so grateful.'

We raised a glass and toasted merrily.

After the meal we retired to my folks' place. I hadn't opened my gifts yet. I dropped down onto mum's rug and began tearing at the shiny paper. There were lots of lovely things. But the final gift was a winner. I removed the glossy wrap to reveal a cool white box about fourteen inches in length. My heart flipped. It was a new laptop.

My folks had invested in everything I would need to make music for the next couple of years, including a great microphone. It was a challenge in many ways. I was now in a position to start demoing some of the songs I'd started to write. And that's just what I did.

In the weeks that followed I became absorbed in my new toys. It was difficult at first. There are few things worse for your artistic flow than having to read through pages and pages of wordy instructions. But I began to make headway after a while. After lifting the clean white machine from its pristine packaging I set things up in the spare room. There I was again – just like in my teens. But this time I had something much deeper, far more profound to say. I began to record the new songs.

WASHED

ONE SUNDAY, Andrew Seaton (who I'd forgiven at this point for challenging me to 'take off the old me' just weeks earlier) announced that there was going to be a baptismal service at church. He appealed for anyone who'd found faith but not yet had a water baptism to put their name down. I signed up.

It happened that the baptism day fell on Easter Sunday. The Bishop of Yorkshire was going to come to perform the service. Leading up to the event I had a sense of unease at times. It was as though things would pop up to distract me from attending church. I invited both Mum and Dad to the service. I felt that it would be good for them to see where I was spending so much of my time. My dad declined, much to my disappointment, but I had to respect his views.

On the day of the baptism I felt a little off-centre. Roo came to Sheffield to watch the service and my mum came along too. She sweetly brought gifts of a pendant and bracelet with scriptural engraving. One read, 'I can do all things through Christ who strengthens me' (Philippians 4:13 NKJV) and the other, '"Not by might nor by power but by my spirit" says the Lord' (Zechariah 4:6 NKJV).

That morning while I got ready I looked one last time at my little New Testament. I opened it at random to find this passage:

A Call to Persevere in Faith

Therefore . . . since we have confidence to enter the Most Holy Place by the blood of Jesus, by a new and living way opened for us through the curtain, that is, his body, and since we have a great priest over the house of God, let us draw near to God with a sincere heart in full assurance of faith, having our hearts sprinkled to cleanse us from a guilty conscience and having our bodies washed with pure water (Hebrews 10:19–22).

I was impressed with my find. The passage seemed to sum up what I was about to undertake.

When it came to the baptism I was quite nervous. I lined up alongside my friends as one by one they were taken into the large inflatable pool and dunked by the bishop.

I was one of the last to go. I looked out to the packed church and got into the pool. The water was lukewarm and reached to my knees. I confessed my faith. With Andy Rushworth on one side and the Bishop on the other I was dunked three times and raised back up. The congregation cheered!

Afterward, I broke my Lenten chocolate fast with a biscuit and went to talk to my mum. I felt relieved. I'd made it to a public confession of faith.

Before I left church that day, I picked up a Bible and flicked it open. It was an old Bible, the full deal not just the New Testament.

To my amazement it fell open to the same passage I had read that morning. It was a different book with different page numbers, yet of all the passages, the same one sat in front of me.

I felt a sense of completion.

HEARTBREAK

DATING ROO was bittersweet. We were like two peas in a fluorescent pod and wherever we went, fun was sure to follow. But since the day we became an item, I had a sense of disquiet in my soul. I felt it was inevitable that the relationship wouldn't last.

After a couple of weeks when several signs hinted at us fizzling out, we had a late night conversation. I don't know if we were really fizzling. I think I just feared we were and recoiled all warmth as a defence mechanism. It was a technique I learned at school: never show a person how you really feel. It totally freaks them out and makes you vulnerable. A counter-productive approach perhaps.

Roo and I were great at being friends. A summary of our time together would be a picture of us driving, listening to our favourite music and missing the turn-off because of the best moments in the song.

We could talk about anything except what was going on between us. The mystery was always the central feature. I never really knew what was going on. It was always gauged by the 'vibe'.

This particular conversation was typical of our relationship. A lyric-fest of riddles and hints. It was an indirect and cryptic conversation.

'I don't know how you feel to be honest,' Roo said in a slightly irritated tone.

'Well, to be honest I don't know how I feel either.'

'I don't think we're really falling for each other in that way.'

'Obviously not,' I spat. We sat in silence for some time. It was late. Roo began to drift into some kind of sleep. I went to bed.

Once I had settled in bed my heart broke. Lying in the spare room the thing in my chest tore in two. I sobbed. Flashes of the preceding months charged through my ribcage like a stampede. For the first time I could feel the hurt of breaking up with Hugh. There was a strange loss to that. I wanted to be as far from him as possible but there was still a space where his love, his friends and my life with him had been. Until that moment my attention had settled on the new things in my life. But lying in the bed I felt the full force of both break-ups. It was a double whammy. Meeting Roo had turned my life upside down. I didn't regret it. But things certainly seemed to be up in the air between us now.

I was becoming someone whom I had to get to know afresh. I reached for my Bible and flicked to Philippians 4:13: 'I can do all things through Christ who strengthens me' (NKJV).

I awoke the next morning and the break-up sting hit me afresh. Had it been one of those unwelcome but ever-so-real anxiety dreams? No. The conversation really had taken place. Neither of us had really called it, but there was no need. We knew the relationship was over. As he dropped me at the station that morning Preston looked grey.

As we parted I couldn't muster a smile. I was tired from a year of change and heartbreak. On the train platform the emotions bubbled. Preston train station was haunted with memories.

I began to cry like a baby. The normal self-control that being in public demands did not apply to me that day, I didn't care who saw me. I could feel the sick and unwelcome stares of concerned strangers. I could almost hear the silent enquiries of suited commuters behind laptops, 'What's up love? What could be so bad?' The sobs of the broken-hearted inspire natural empathy.

From here I began to forge a *new*, new life. It was going to be tough. But when I thought about it, I'd been in a relationship for most of my teen years. It made sense that I should get to know myself without a significant other.

THE PURPLE TIGHTS

THAT WEEKEND I went to stay at my sister's cosy house in Lepton for the first time in a while. I was in a bit of a strange mood. You never quite feel yourself when you've just broken up with someone, even if the circumstances have been good.

I woke up on Saturday morning feeling out of sorts. I thought about all the God stuff. Had I just been imaging it all? Was it all just a part of the romance between Roo and me? I was terrified that now Roo was out of the picture God would disappear too.

As I stirred in my sister's spare bed I thought about a party I had coming up the following week. I had been searching for some purple tights for a certain outfit (don't ask) but had no idea where I'd find them. I also had a very tight budget (excuse the pun). So I threw down the gauntlet once again to God.

'God, if you are there, I would really appreciate a sign. I want to be sure that this relationship is real and I haven't just been living off Roo's faith. God, if you're there please find me some purple tights for under a fiver.'

It sounds daft now, but at the time I figured it was a sufficient challenge. Needless to say, purple tights weren't the most common thing in those days and you'd most likely pay over the odds if you found some in a specialist boutique.

My sister and I went into town shopping that day. She had shoes to buy for Lucy and January sales to scour. We looked around, had a bit of lunch and drank some coffee. I was still looking for my tights.

At the last minute I popped into a discount store on the high street. I had a quick scout around and couldn't see any hosiery. Then, at the last moment, in the corner of my eye I spotted a cardboard bargain bin filled with all kinds of bits and bobs. Belts, purses, single socks, broken necklaces and novelty key rings.

'Wouldn't it just be funny if . . .' I thought as I began to rummage. I spotted a pair of green fishnets that were plastic-wrapped around a cardboard insert. I was excited – if they had green fishnets then maybe they would have . . . and there they were. Purple fishnet tights in perfect condition for £2. God had bettered me! He'd beaten my budget and provided exactly what I asked for.

It was only a pair of tights – no big deal. But what it meant to my broken heart that day was something more. God was there, he was watching, and he could do absolutely anything, no matter how big or small. I felt at peace.

PART 3
INTO THE CLEARING

FIREWORKS

OON AFTER I had decided to move to Sheffield I told Steph what I was planning. She was really excited.

'Nick and I are in the process of buying a house. You could come and live with us,' she said. Nick was Steph's close friend and I'd met him several times by now. In fact, he'd been there at church the night I first prayed for Jesus to turn up. He was a musician, break-dancer, DJ and singer with crazy red hair and a very colourful dress-sense. He was a fearless fireball with a great personal confidence.

'That would be amazing! I don't have a lot of money at the moment though,' I said. 'I'm still doing the odd social club gig but I need to get a job really. I really do think Sheffield's the place for me though.'

'Yay. You should come over and spend the night to try it out.'

So I did. I took my overnight bag and chose the small bedroom upstairs. It looked out onto a lovely garden.

After a fun evening eating together and chatting I felt so at ease. I loved the church Nick and Steph were part of and I loved its social culture. The way everyone treated each other and the way they talked about God like he was family appealed to me. They both made me laugh. I found that whenever we sat down to chat I always forgot my problems.

Nick and Steph offered to let me move in at a tiny rate of rent, and even made a shiny purple envelope saying 'rent fairy', which they stuck to the pantry wall to help me feel less awkward about paying to be there.

A couple of weeks later with next to no money (some serious debt in fact), no furniture and no job I moved in. As I put my possessions in the little bedroom I started to feel an incredible sense of calm.

That night we had a meal together and drank a couple of bottles of beer. We went out onto the decking and the three of us huddled up under a blanket. As we sat there suddenly a huge fireworks' display began.

'Where's that coming from?' Steph squealed.

'Must be the local pub,' explained Nick.

'No, that's not the direction of the pub. It must be in someone's garden. It's a massive display.'

We never did work out where the fireworks were coming from, but I knew what I thought. It was a big confirmation that I was doing the right thing. It was a 'welcome home'.

CHEST OF DRAWERS

MY NEW ROOM had very little furniture. There was a laundry chest belonging to Nick. Steph had kindly thrown a purple scarf over it, to make it feel more homely. I went to Argos and spent my last tenner on some flat-pack drawers for underneath the bed. I crammed most of my clothes into the drawers but wasn't able to fit many more things in.

A couple of days after moving Nick and Steph decided to drive me out to Hathersage for a drink. We went on a walk in the Peaks and did a little charity-shop shopping, which was fast becoming the new high street for me.

As we sat outside taking in the fabulous view of the Peaks, Nick noticed something.

'We should have a look in that skip over there. It looks like it's full of goodies.'

'Oh yeah,' said Steph. 'Looks exciting.' We went over to see. The guys found a few bits for the house, picture frames and other odds and ends. But then we noticed something even better. Standing by the skip was a pine chest of drawers.

'Phil – these would be perfect for your room,' Nick said.

I looked them over. They were solid wood and were certainly better than a suitcase.

We chucked them in the back of the car and took them home. After wiping them down and taking a few old toys out, we found that they were perfect. I put the chest of drawers in my room and stuck a few picture frames and bottles of perfume on top. They were perfect.

I couldn't believe I'd managed to find some furniture. These days it seemed that I was always in the right place at the right time.

And, better still, I hadn't had to use a credit card.

Job on the Doorstep

A FEW DAYS after settling in at the new house, I set about trying to find work. I was still doing the odd gig at a pub or working men's club, but I needed something more stable so I didn't have to rely on my parents for back-up.

Nick and I walked down Chesterfield Road. It was quite a charming street. There were a couple of pubs, a chemist or two, a video store and an unusually vast array of charity shops.

We walked down the long road, asking in every shop for vacancies. It seemed too much to ask to find work so close to home, but it was worth a shot. Finally, right as the shops thinned out towards the back end of the road we came across Venture. It was a high-end portrait studio and on the door there was a sign:

Job vacancies. Telesales position full-time Monday to
Thursday 1–9 p.m.
No experience needed as all training given.

Wow, a day job that started after lunch sounded right up my street. We pressed the bell and asked to see Beverly (the duty manager). She came out of nowhere dressed sharply in a tailored trouser suit. She had spiky cropped hair and a glint in her eye. I thought she'd have no interest in someone like me, but to my surprise she was very keen.

'Well you seem confident and friendly, probably due to your music job,' she said breezily. 'Can you start on Monday?'

I was over the moon. I found out the job paid more than the minimum wage and there were sales bonuses up for grabs too. Nick and I celebrated with Steph that evening.

Soul Survivor

I T WAS a couple of weeks after the break-up and I was still in a bit of a funk. I hoped a little sun and sea would help. I was booked on another family holiday. A year to the month after my Hale miracle I went to Greece with the folks. My sister and baby niece came too. But I didn't feel right for the whole holiday. I felt so out of place in my own family. I waded into the sea looking up towards the mountains and prayed.

'God, help lift me out of this. I'm just not feeling right. Restore unto me the joy of my salvation! Fill me with the Holy Spirit.' I felt I was searching, chasing. I was trying so hard to have fun and be happy. I guess in truth I was still nursing a broken heart. I bobbed along in the silky saltwater staring at the clear blue sky.

'Here I am in this gorgeous place and I just feel so low,' I said aloud, a nearby lilo-bather eyeing me in confusion. 'God I think I'm being a terrible witness to my family.'

At that stage I was so self-conscious about my family's view of me. I felt they thought I was a crazy Christian. My disposition on this trip was not helping my case. Yeah, here I am all saved and healed and whole everybody – sorry, I'm also completely miserable!

There were a couple of awkward conversations that made me feel even more estranged. They were picking up on my vibe and they weren't impressed.

Floating out on the water, alone but for the gentle waves and the presence of God, I prayed and prayed. But it didn't feel like it was working. I'd babble away searching for some sound within my soul that would release the heaviness. The break-up with Roo had left stones in my spirit. I felt lost. Why was I in Sheffield? Had I just followed a boy into church and derailed myself? Was it all a big illusion that was distancing me from my family and my chosen career? There was a gaping hole in my life where Roo's friendship had been. So much light and life had grown from him.

On top of that, my voice was suffering. It was dry and sore and disappearing. I wasn't sleeping well.

As soon as I returned to the UK I had another trip to go on. I had booked myself onto something called Soul Survivor with Nick and Steph.

I wasn't sure what to expect from this Christian festival. I half-expected they'd see straight through me and into the darkness that still seemed to encircle every day. After the four-hour journey I fell out of the car and onto the campsite.

Students were everywhere. I couldn't help thinking it was one huge date-a-thon – a great place to search for a future wife or husband. Could it be him? The curly-haired skater? The tall boy in the white T? To me, they all looked delicious.

'There she is,' came a voice, 'looking very sun-kissed.' It was Roo, setting up camp. He was being kind but my heart went cold. I was still hurt.

That night I joined the heavy throng of young people making for the main meeting venue. It was a giant cowshed; a huge space brimming with tanned young people all with Bibles in hand. There were youth Bibles, metal Bibles,

Message Bibles, Bibles in bags, Bibles concordances, red-lettering, mission Bibles . . . you get the gist.

The worship began and music washed out over the crowd. I looked at the stage. The sound was flawless. I knew most of the songs – we had sung them at church. Tim Hughes was leading. Roo had played me one of Tim's CDs ages ago. 'He's really talented,' I'd mocked. 'It's a shame it's just Jesus music. He could make a killing in mainstream music.'

Now there he was – the star attraction. I searched his demeanour for arrogance, but there was none. I searched the crowd for sycophancy, there seemed to be none. Instead I saw a thousand pairs of smooth young arms raised up, a thousand pairs of closed eyes. The music pulsated across the gathering. As the band swelled and waned the voices were the honorary band-member. It was the leaders' week and within that gathering there must have been hundreds of worship leaders. The harmony sounded angelic, and just as had happened in that room with Ric's dad leading worship, I began to drift into the glorious sound. But the pain in my throat prevented me singing along. It felt like a blockage between me and God. If I wasn't able to sing, how could I be a part of this?

The meeting drew to a close. I chatted to Steph afterwards. I told her how I was feeling and she sympathized. But it was as if the whirlwind of Soul Survivor had her wrapped up. It was like the world was whirling around me in a contented haze and I was still, motionless, looking on. As I lay in my tent the chorus 'Our God Is an Awesome God' went round and round in my mind, soothing me, and I fell asleep.

The nights that followed were similar. I wrestled with the experience. Then one night, things seemed to change again.

We went into the cowshed and Delirious? were playing. The worship was powerful. During the meeting Martin Smith encouraged us to pray for one another. I started to pray – first for Ben, then for Nick. As I was praying the hardness in my core began to melt. The heaviness began to move and crackle. With my hand on a stranger's shoulder I began to pray aloud, my heart filling with compassion for this person I'd never met. But there was a slight disquiet. I kept thinking, 'There must be another person here I should be praying for.' I moved through the crowd praying as I went. Then I felt the urge to move my hand away from anyone at all. A familiar voice spoke into my ear. It was Roo.

'Philippa, I think God is really doing something in you.' Fear struck me as I considered this. I certainly did feel something. A bubbling warmth within. It felt like pain and peace about to collide – like an oozing, fizzing sensation moving outward from my core. I wasn't really aware what was happening, but other people had noticed.

Before I knew it, several hands were on my shoulders. I was kind of crying, but not in the usual sense. It was more like a sobbing from the spirit, as if all my angst was surfacing, rippling through my belly and outwards. Strangers spoke gentle prayers over me. It was like being emptied and filled at the same time. As I cried in a heap I felt suffering leave and peace settle. I had a sudden thought, 'I'm exchanging my hurt for songs.'

As I looked around the room after the meeting it was as if a strange veil had been lifted once again. I bounced around chatting to people as if I'd just thawed from some terrible, frozen state. And afterwards, as I spoke to Roo we both noticed it. I felt comfortable being friends with him from that point on.

I slept like a baby that night. All my guilt and shame had lifted, as had all my feelings of being not good enough. I felt secure and accepted by God. It was like this huge reminder that he cared. He had touched my heart and healed something.

Days later my voice returned. It was stronger than before.

Holy Dove?

THE SOCIAL CLUB scene is a British phenomenon. Local working men pay fees to be members of a private social club. The beer is cheap and everyone knows each other's names. In the sixties and seventies the scene was at its peak. Women and families came into the mix, and on a weekend the clubs would always book entertainment. This is how my Dad made his pennies over the decades.

When I started on the circuit I had plenty of bookings. But I always found it hard to choose the right repertoire of songs. I chose what I thought was a broad selection, but looking back, it was far too contemporary. I should have just chosen songs I knew they'd like. But I was young and wanted to prove myself.

When I became a Christian, I started looking for a deeper meaning in the songs and it made these gigs more enjoyable. It worked really well for 'Say a Little Prayer'. I even introduced that song as being about Jesus a few times (much to my dad's complete embarrassment). One night, this inspired a surprise reaction.

After my first set, I came down through the side door of the dressing room and out into the club. An older chap came over to speak to me.

'Oh dear,' I thought. 'I must have murdered one of his favourite songs.' But to my complete surprise the response was deep and profound.

'You're a Christian you, aren't ya?' he asked in clipped Yorkshire tones. I shrunk a little.

'Yeah, I am.' He looked around as if to see whether anyone was looking over his shoulder.

'These lot in 'ere don't get it,' he said. At this point I was beginning to get worried, but he continued, 'It's because the name of Jesus pierces their heart. Because it's truth, and they're not ready for the truth.'

I was totally taken aback. I had only mentioned Jesus once. No preaching and no sharing of the gospel. All I'd said was his name!

'This is your ministry,' he added.

Social clubs are usually so predictable: the same format of songs and beers on tap. This moment was a total departure from the norm. The man pointed to his glass of beer.

'This is not very Christian,' he said, slurring a little, 'but I'm back-slidden.' I'd heard this term a few times. It was a term Christians used to describe other Christians who had stopped seeking God and regressed to their old habits.

I didn't know what to say.

'It's alright,' I stuttered. 'No one's perfect.'

'Then there's me wife,' he was in full swing now. 'We're having big problems with our eldest son and me wife just can't stop crying.'

I went over to his wife, who indeed was crying into her drink.

'Awe, what's up?' I asked.

'It's me son. He's having awful problems and I just feel like I'm under a massive spiritual attack.'

I shot a glance at my friend who had driven me to the show that night as if to say, 'See, this is what happens when you start talking about Jesus.'

The husband returned and asked me, 'Will you pray for us like?'

So I did. On my way out of the venue I stretched out an arm to this couple and prayed. I could never have imagined I would end up praying for strangers in a working men's club.

As I grew in faith, my attitude towards audiences really started to change. I started to see myself not just as a performer, but also as a servant. It says in the Bible that Jesus came not to be served but to serve. I wanted to apply this. Rather than looking out and seeing a bunch of moody faces staring back at me, I began to see people who just wanted to feel something. They wanted to let go, have fun, and hear songs they loved. When it comes down to it, everyone has similar basic human needs.

One evening, I found myself in a particularly lovely social club. I was singing away and came to the fail-safe classic, 'Close to you' by The Carpenters. Though I didn't say it out loud, I began to pray inwardly, 'God, I want to feel that you're close. I want to know that you're there, and I want to feel safe in you. Wouldn't it be great for the people in this room to catch a glimpse of you?'

Just as I began to sing the line about birds suddenly appearing, the craziest thing happened. There was a bit of a commotion at one side of the room. I thought they were laughing at my song choice, or my voice or something, but I was wrong. A bird had flown into the club! It flew around for almost the entire song before it was eventually cornered near an open window and ushered out. A bird suddenly appeared – unbelievable.

You really can't make this stuff up!

GLASTONBURY

I STARTED WORK at the portrait studio and took to it like a duck to water. Despite putting on a few pounds from sitting at a desk eight hours a day and snacking on endless M&Ms, I enjoyed the job. It was pretty easy: call people, tell them they've won a free portrait session and send them info. I loved sending out the info. I felt like a proper grown-up. But under the surface I was desperately hoping to find some more opportunities in music – my true passion.

Not long into the job I had a call from Mum.

'I've just seen something on Calendar you might be interested in,' she said. Ever my biggest supporter, Mum was always on the lookout for musical opportunities for me.

'There's a band that's been booked for Glastonbury and their singer has had to drop out due to the birth of her baby. They're auditioning for a replacement,' she told me.

I was excited. I'd always dreamed of playing at Glastonbury. Mum said that the band would be auditioning singers at a venue in Barnsley. I grew more excited. As I hung up the phone I danced around the kitchen praying aloud, 'God I really want this! Please sort this one out for me and I promise I'll give you glory!' It was interesting. As I prayed, I really felt as if I was going to my dad and asking him to pull strings. I had an odd feeling I had this one in the bag.

On the day of the auditions there were two areas: a lit stage facing a table of judges, and a waiting area filled with expectant female singers of all kinds. I caught a glimpse of someone doing a great rendition of 'Black Velvet'.

Since picking up the guitar I had written half a dozen new songs, but at this stage I wasn't very confident playing them. I'd been playing the songs to Roo and he'd been helping create the parts. He'd then played them for me to demo to.

I brought Roo's guitar demo to sing to at the audition. I knew it was a risk to bring a blatantly Christian song, but I figured that – if nothing else – I wanted to brighten up the audition room.

My turn came and I took to the stage. As Roo's guitar demo started, I threw caution to the wind and started to sing. I closed my eyes and put all my heart and energy and passion into delivering the song. I focused on the moment. The judges thanked me for my performance and I left.

I went home feeling really confident about the experience. Several hours later I had a phone call. It was the band's front man.

'Hi Philippa! We really enjoyed your audition today. It was very different from the others, and we'd really like to invite you to play with us at Glastonbury.' I did a silent scream on the other end of the phone and skipped around the room like a crazy kid.

'That's amazing. I'm so pleased. Wow, thank you so much.'

'No worries. You were our clear favourite. So, we need to arrange a rehearsal time for you to come and learn the songs.'

I was over the moon and after a little diary consultation we scheduled a song-learning session at the front man's house on the other side of town. It was a total answer to prayer. It seemed amazing that after unashamedly singing about Jesus at an audition I'd sailed through it and risen to the top of the pile. I felt that God had been with me and had given me confidence.

A few days later the guitarist from the band came to fetch me and we went to listen to the music with a couple of the band members.

'So, this is our most popular song, and this one really relies on the female vocal. Have a listen.' He fired up his hi-fi and the song began to play. I wasn't sure about the style; it wasn't like anything I'd done before, but I decided to keep an open mind. As I continued to listen my heart dropped a little further.

'Erm, what is this song about?' I asked a little sheepishly. The guys looked at one another.

'Well, you could take it a few ways really, but it's kind of a tongue in cheek song about smoking weed.'

At that moment I realized that this was an opportunity I was going to have to pass up on.

'Guys, I feel really bad about this. Maybe I should have said something sooner, but I didn't realize there was going to be this kind of content. Oh, this is awkward . . .' I could see the realization sweeping over them. They knew what I was getting at.

We talked it through and they were totally cool about my decision. I was, to all intents and purposes, a youth leader now and the last thing I wanted to do was to encourage pot smoking.

The guys understood and after a last ditch attempt to convince me by showing me a Christian cannabis lovers' website, they drove me home. I had total peace about the situation.

I thought afterwards about this 'miraculous opportunity' that turned out to be false. It seemed that God had sailed me through that audition process. I had got what I asked for. But more importantly I'd learned that I had new boundaries. It wasn't worth compromising my principles just for the sake of a show.

I believed that God would open the right doors for me at the right time.

All Bar One

I DID my best at the portrait studio. I worked overtime and slogged my guts out on the phones. But for whatever reason it wasn't really working out. After an amicable conversation with Bev we came to the conclusion that 'I wasn't telesales material' and she let me go. It was time to look for another job. Thankfully, with the odd gig at weekends I was still managing to pay the 'rent-fairy', but money was getting a little thin on the ground.

I printed out my CV. It wasn't very impressive. I'd done OK in my favourite subjects at school (even if I had been suspended once for writing a rude poem). I had a little experience of bar work and a bit of retail. But, having spent the last couple of years pursuing music, my work experience was sparse.

I trawled the web for jobs. I liked people and shopping so naturally I applied for Boots, Topshop and the like (anywhere with a favourable discount opportunity and interaction with the general public). A couple of weeks passed and nothing emerged. I filled out countless applications online. Nothing.

Eventually, I knew it was time. If the job wasn't going to come to me, I'd have to go to the job. So, I went out on foot with a bunch of CVs in my bag and began looking for work. In all fairness, this was arguably my first encounter with the 'real world'. I was out in the big city trying to find something – anything – that might keep me there.

As I wandered through the bustling autumn streets, busy with a rainbow of students, I held one thought in mind, 'Lord, I'll do anything except waitressing.' Surely God wouldn't send me into a job I didn't want to do, would he?

After a tough day of hearing 'We're fully staffed, thanks,' and 'We're not recruiting at the moment,' I turned the corner into Orchard Square. It seemed that all the retail jobs had gone to attractive students in leg-warmers. I was running out of bright shop fronts to approach. Then I saw it. Before me lay the most intimidating bar I could imagine. It had a whole wall of different wines. Staff were actually climbing ladders to retrieve Pinot Noir and it was terrifying to watch. They were wearing crisp white shirts and wielding arms full of tapas plates. But before I knew it, I'd walked right in.

Propped at the bar hatch poring over what looked like a rota was Matt, a short, red-haired manager with trendy brown shoes and a matching belt.

I pulled my shoulders back and prayed that my blonde hair still had the power it carried before Jesus.

'Hi there,' I chirped. His blue eyes glittered as I approached with my crisp CV shivering under the air con. 'Just wondering if you have any hours going?'

He smiled, 'Yeah, we have as a matter of fact.' He was quick and snappy.

'Have you got bar experience?'

'Yeah, I've worked in a hotel actually, doing functions and that sort of thing. I worked at the local pub too.' (I left out the fact that I'd barely taken a dish from the kitchen.)

'Brilliant. We'll get you in for an interview. Thursday OK for you? Andy's on so he'll sort you out.'

I couldn't believe my ears. We exchanged details and I left with a smile.

Thursday came around and I dressed to impress. I wore my black trouser suit (the one I often wore for club gigs) and made the effort to blow dry and straighten my hair.

As I approached the proud glass doors I wondered what was happening – the bar looked closed. But I pushed the door and it opened.

'Erm, we're not actually open yet,' came a voice with an Irish accent. It belonged to yet another redhead, Giles, who was casually pouring ice into the sinks.

'Oh, that's OK, I'm here for an interview. Are you the manager?'

Giles shrugged, 'I wish. He's cleaning the lines. I'll go and get him.'

Moments later Andy emerged from the staircase. He was attractive, though definitely not dressed to impress.

'Sorry, I didn't realize I had an interview to do today,' he said in his jovial Liverpool brogue. 'I've been sorting the cellar out, I must look like a right scrubber.' I liked him immediately.

'Yeah, sorry, Matt said you were interviewing me at eleven.'

'No worries. Have a seat. Would you like a drink?'

'Water please.' I don't know why I said that. I could really have done with a coffee. I guess I wanted to appear low maintenance.

'So, do you have bar experience?'

I answered his questions and he kept saying, 'Great, great' and ticked off boxes on a form.

'So, you're a singer it says here?'

'Yes. I write songs too. But I need a real job at the moment,' I smiled. 'I'm looking for something that's flexible and fun.'

'What brings you to Sheffield then?'

'I just joined a church actually. I've been working with a youth ministry in Ecclesall.'

His eyebrows raised, 'You don't know Joel Toombs do you?'

'Yes I do – he's my friend's brother-in-law.' His face lit up.

'I used to play football with him! Great guy. Yeah, well, if you're alright with them you're alright with me!'

'I should tell you, I haven't really had much waitressing experience.'

'Don't worry, it's not rocket science. You're obviously switched on. I'm sure you'll be fine.'

I walked out of the interview with a job. It was amazing. And not least because in the three years that followed at All Bar One, I never once saw anyone offered a job at the first hurdle.

BULLSEYE

I'VE NEVER been very lucky. I've never really won anything – only a huge teddy at the circus one time, and even that turned out to be flammable. With my music it had felt like I'd been dealt one low card after another. Demos returned marked, 'Try again next year'. 'Not my cup of tea' was a favourite of mine. There were even local pub karaoke competitions where I didn't make the top three and one where I had to accept my consolation prize as the winner line-danced her way tunelessly through Shania Twain.

And then there was the TV show. 'And the winner is . . . Leanne!' I can still feel the cold volts of disappointment in my belly if I think about it for long enough. And the auditions in London for which my mum bought me an entire sports' shop (no one needs that many sports bras). I gave my all, my best, and my name was never called.

After that kind of run of bad luck (or bad performances, God only knows) I had learned to feel like a bit of a loser. I wasn't naturally miserable but I had learned to accept and expect failure. But it seemed things were finally looking up.

As I read the Bible I began to find verses about God's favour. There were also lots of verses about God's kindness and God giving good gifts.

When Nick's band, The Gentlemen, decided to hire a 1,000-seater venue for their album launch we all breathed a unified, 'They'll never fill that.' Nicholas, with the grace of a true gentleman retorted, 'I've got God's favour. Always have had.'

Now don't get me wrong, there is such a thing as a spoiled child. But I think we've lost sight of a deeper truth. We were made to expect kindness from our parents. It's supposed to be a given.

So, I became an advocate for God's favour. I began to confess at every opportunity that God was my father and that he would give me the desires of my heart. People often laugh when I pray for everyday miracles, even praying during board games.

'You can't do that,' said Steph one Christmas. 'We're all Christians. Why should God help you to win?'

'Well, I don't hear you praying.' I answered. The following 'miracle' came after a moment like that.

I was visiting a friend, Ben. He wasn't just any friend mind you. He was a close, best, past-boyfriend type of friend. After leaving school we became inseparable and only lost touch when I moved away to Preston.

I went to visit. Ben's room was just the same as it had always been: tidy, slightly nerdy, but beautifully representing the lad he was. It was clean but mildly cluttered with his collection of real ale bottles and bits of computer paraphernalia. Bob Marley and Anna Kournicova shared the walls.

As we sat in his room catching up, I began to talk about God. Although I don't remember the conversation too well, it was eclipsed by what happened next. He picked up his darts and began aiming. He was pretty good at it really. (But then you should be good at any game that is stuck to your bedroom wall.)

He was chattering away as he threw each dart, expressing his atheism. The next thing I knew he'd passed me the darts and I stood up to take a shot.

Now I'm quite a girly girl. I shouldn't be allowed to hold something like a dart without adult supervision. My aim is atrocious, no, laughable. I took a shot and was met with hearty laughter. I think it just about made the board, though not the *scoring* part of the board.

'Now wait a minute,' I said coolly, 'I know I can do this with Jesus onside.' The remark was partly tongue-in-cheek, an ice-breaking poke at my own Bible-bashing. But at the same time I believed what I had said.

'Go on then. If God's real then get a bullseye.' My eyes lit up.

'Will you believe in God if I get a bullseye right now?' He laughed again.

'Yes. A resounding yes!' The gauntlet was down. I took aim and looked clean down the dart's glistening blue stem.

'Come on Jesus. You heard Ben, you'd better make this happen,' I prayed silently. I had complete confidence. This was not my battle, not my dart.

Ready . . . aim . . . BULLSEYE!

It was like it happened in slow motion. I looked again. Yes, it had hit the very centre of that dartboard. I'd never seen a cleaner bullseye.

'No way!' Ben shouted. 'I can't believe it! You must have cheated. How far away were you?'

Ben didn't confess faith in Christ that night. But my faith grew one dart-length more.

LET'S START A BAND

INVOLVEMENT AT The Anvil in Sheffield was quite full on. It was more of a lifestyle than a youth group. There were always a dozen things going on. Andy Rushworth was a revolutionary. He had a gift for envisioning young people that I've never seen before. He didn't just get people to do things; he ignited a vision in each of us that together we could change the world.

Andy also held another great vision in his hands, that of unity in the church. He initiated something that embodied this in the form of citywide leaders' meetings. The meetings were held at Montgomery Hall and we all tried to attend each month.

Montgomery Hall was situated in the centre of town. It was an old building just off the high street that had been active since the thirties with everything from opera to lectures and conferences. The building was owned by the church and was often used to house plays and productions.

The meetings were in an upper room away from any of the excitement.

The first time I went in there it seemed pretty similar to the other church meetings, except that the congregation was a hotchpotch of leaders from all around Sheffield. Several familiar faces would always be there. A church leader named Baz was always present. It turned out he had hosted that very first event where I prayed the prayer. Josh and Joel, the brothers whom we'd met at the studio were there too.

On my very first visit to the monthly gathering Pete Dawson led us in some songs to open the meeting. He was a young graduate who'd studied drums at a Christian college. He had a great voice and he played guitar well. He certainly seemed to have a real passion for God. After the meeting Andy came over.

'I think it would be really good for you to work with Pete. He's a great drummer. His brother Tim plays bass too,' he explained.

The comment went over my head a little. I'd never really had any involvement with a band. The thought actually terrified me a little – all those musicians surrounding my voice. It seemed like too much fuss to surround little old me with a band.

A couple of moments later, a second bespectacled gentleman approached me and we began chatting. He looked like Pete but was a couple of years older. He had a similar polite energy and was a little less surfy.

'Hi Philippa, I'm Tim. Andy says you'd be up for a bit of a jam sometime?'

'Yeah, that seems to be the plan,' I said, feeling a little overwhelmed.

'Great. We'll be in touch. I think Andy has all your details. We'll be in touch,' he repeated, smiling gently. I couldn't quite believe that musicians would be so keen to work with me.

Weeks later, Andy arranged the first practice session. I was fraught with nerves. It was a Saturday morning and I was exhausted. This just seemed like another thing to add to the madness of my busy life. But at the same time, the practice session sizzled in the dark autumn morning like a weak flicker of hope for my music. After so much disappointment I hardly dared hope that it would become something significant.

Andy Baker took charge. He taught the boys the structures and chords. I just sang. I only had a handful of songs: 'Crazy Days', an ode to my old life that I'd recorded gingerly in Mum and Dad's spare room, 'Watching Me' and 'Father'. It all went well and I was very impressed with the boys. They certainly did play well together.

'Wow,' I thought. 'So this is what it feels like to have someone play your songs.'

At the end of the practice Andy excitedly began to talk about when we would meet again.

'You just need some more songs now Philippa. Are you working on anything new?'

'I do have a new song on the go . . .' I offered, hoping I wouldn't be asked to play it.

'Can you play a little bit of it?' asked Pete. Pete has a way that puts you right at ease. For a moment I sort of believed I could play guitar in front of them. I picked up the acoustic. My body stiffened and my mouth went dry. My heart pounded as I began to pick out the chords. I sang barely above a whisper, highly self-conscious about my naive attempt at Christian lyrics. I spat out half a verse and chorus before throwing the guitar back towards Andy, my cheeks flushed.

'That's really cool. Yeah we'll definitely do that one next time.'

JOEL

AT THAT TIME I wasn't in any rush to find love. I'd always believed that you should follow your emotions, but as I read the Scriptures I stumbled upon some incredible wisdom. Romance should never be a distraction. It should enrich your life and help you move forward with God's plan, rather than hold you back.

The New Testament actually championed being single, which I found a little scary at first. There's so much you can do and focus on without the distraction of a love interest. But it also recommended marriage. Marriage is the beginning of a new family.

I decided that I wouldn't date anyone until I thought there might be a chance I could marry them. I never dreamed that that person would be just around the corner.

A little time passed and I heard that my housemate Nick had formed a band with Josh, Joel and Sean. Sean was the guitarist from the worship band at The Anvil. I was so excited; I knew they'd be good. But when I heard their rough demos I was more impressed than I'd expected to be. Nick had real star quality and in this context he really shone. The band was outstanding and the songs were really shaping up too.

The band frequently came round to hang out at our place. They'd sit with us and watch old movies. They'd shake the house with their rehearsals in the basement and have drawn-out tea-drinking sessions in the afternoons.

One evening we had a bonfire in the garden. Nick gathered a heap of old furniture and twigs and set the blaze going. I hung out in the kitchen while Steph was cooking. Joel struck up a rare conversation with me.

'So you've done some dance music, is that right?' I was pleasantly surprised at his speaking voice.

'Er, yeah a couple of things.'

'Finding You?' he jumped in (this was a song I'd recorded years earlier).

'Yes, how did you know?'

'I found it online.' Hmmm, I thought. Googling me hey? Can't be bad.

'Oh, wow,' I said, flattered.

'That's cool,' someone else joined in, 'have you got any songs on CD?' I thought for a second.

'I think I have some demos hanging around.'

'I'd love a demo,' Joel chimed in, with a mysterious glint in his eyes. I was pleasantly intrigued.

'Well I guess I'll have to find you one then,' I replied.

Soon afterwards The Gentlemen began to play local gigs in Sheffield. They were going down a storm. When groups of us went to see them it was electric. It was the passion of the kids from church out in the gritty music scene across the city. They were vibrant young guys performing without aggression, swearing or inappropriate content. Their musical talent and stage presence was unmistakable. They gained fans quickly.

I remember seeing them play for the first time at The Boardwalk. The place rocked when they opened the set.

That night, for the first time I looked at shy, peaceful characters Joel and Josh and saw something amazing. They were like different people: confident, passionate and magnetic to watch.

I playfully chatted to friends as they played, 'Joel's quite hot when he plays the drums,' I said. They giggled along with me.

Days later, I was down in the basement checking my email and noticed I had an MSN request from Joel. I didn't really use MSN that much, so I was a bit unsure what it was all about. My first thought was that someone had tipped him off about my comment.

I accepted the request and received a short message a few days later. It said: 'Hey Philippa it's Joel. I'm really glad about you moving to Sheffield and I'm really looking forward to getting to know you.' It was short and very sweet.

Nick began playing cupid at that point. Joel seemed to turn up at events I was playing at, and so forth.

Then one day, Joel asked me out on a date. Dating was new to me. I'd *never* done it. My peers were mate-daters. You'd get to know someone as a friend and end up dating them. Going out on an actual date seemed so wholesome and traditional. I felt edgy about it. I wondered what Joel and I would have to talk about. In the few moments we'd had alone, conversation had been quite one-sided. But I was willing to give it a shot. We went for coffee.

'This is totally new to me,' he said as we crossed the road to Starbucks.

'Me too!' I said, though we meant very different things. This was Joel's first date, not just with me, but with anyone.

Ever the obedient pastor's son, he'd endeavoured to do the right thing and wait for 'the one'. No pressure then.

As I expected, there wasn't much conversation. Joel was shy. But he was also very sweet. It amazed me that guys like him still existed. I decided to go on a second date.

Joel drove us out to the Peaks this time. We bought coffees and sat outside the same pub where I had found the chest of drawers with Nick and Steph. After a brief chat, Joel began what sounded like a well-rehearsed speech.

'So, I suppose you're wondering why I brought you out here.' I didn't know what he meant. But I let him finish.

'I just wanted to say. I think that you should be my girlfriend.' It was my turn to be quiet.

'OK. Err, right Joel. I don't really feel like I know you very well.' I fidgeted.

'Right,' he said calmly.

'And I don't know what you know about me, but you're a pastor's son. You've never put a foot wrong in your life. I know you've never had a girlfriend or anything. But I've had boyfriends . . .'

'Yeah I know,' he said.

'Joel, I just don't think I'm good enough for someone like you.' He looked confused.

'Well that's just silly,' he said. 'You're a Christian. I don't care about all that. I've prayed about it and I really feel God saying it's OK.' We looked out to the Peaks again.

'Well Joel, I'm sure you feel like you know me because I talk a lot and stuff. But I feel like I hardly know you.' He brightened up.

'That's totally fine. Let's get to know each other more.'

As we drove back from the Peaks, I played the words over in my mind. Joel drove quietly, peacefully. There was no awkwardness. I felt content.

'I could get used to this feeling,' I thought.

God Scares a Thief

Eventually Joel and I became official. He was good to his word and never made me feel anything other than special. We sort of made up for each other's weaknesses. Joel kept his supportive arm close by at all times.

Our lives were beginning to synchronize too. Joel made a habit of visiting me at work in between his band commitments. We would often stay with each other's parents. It was so cosy and I felt safe. He never pressured me to be anything or do anything. He never made any demands on my time or on my emotions.

One cold Saturday afternoon in the early part of the year Joel and I went to a band practice at church together. It was at All Saints' Church where The Anvil youth service was held each Sunday.

We drove past the inviting roads and up to the back entrance of the church. After parking, we grabbed our practice gear and scurried inside. As I recall, we were running a little late that particular day and had powered down the fairy-tale pathway, guitar and snares in tow, dreading that 'What time do you call this?' look on Andy Baker's face. Thankfully everyone was running late that day.

We set up our things and began the practice. We were all focused on what we were doing when a lady came in, gloves and hat in hand, as though looking for someone. Andy stopped the band.

'Are you alright there?' he asked responsibly.

'Yeah, has somebody got a gold Saxo out the front?' Joel popped his head up from behind the drum-kit.

'Yeah that's me.'

'I'm afraid you've been broken into,' she said in a neighbourly tone. Joel kicked his drum slightly and quickly started for the exit. We followed. Then my heart dropped. Had I left my handbag in the car? I quickly felt for my phone, which to my great relief was in my coat pocket. But everything else was in the bag.

I rushed out to see. The car's passenger door window lay shattered across the car bonnet and sprayed onto the curb like frozen car-tears.

'Did you leave your bag in there?' Joel asked.

'Yeah,' I admitted. In the rush to get into church on time I'd left, not just a handbag, but my overnight bag as well. This contained all of my make-up, toiletries, several items of clothing, jewellery, keys, wallet and even my Bible.

'Oh I can't believe it,' I said. I was panicking. At this stage in my life, I didn't have very much stuff at all. The make-up in that bag was the only stuff I had. I couldn't afford to replace anything.

'I'm going to look for it,' I said frantically. It was strange. I had the oddest feeling that I might find it. 'I know it's around here somewhere,' I thought to myself. I couldn't fight the feeling. I left Joel and Josh kicking glass and calling the police.

I steamed up the road. I'm sure if I'd seen the thief I would have given chase and pleaded for mercy. But I found nothing.

When I returned to the car Joel handed me the phone, 'It's the police. They want to know what was in the bag.'

I described the bag and its contents. We went home and began piecing our lives back together.

'I just can't believe it,' I said. 'Why did God let that happen?' I asked Nick over a brew.

'I'm afraid it's just a fallen world,' Nick said. 'You can't stop people from doing bad things. That's up to them.'

'Well let's just hope the thief reads my Bible and gets saved,' I joked.

About a week later it seemed that my troubles were behind me. I got a new bank card and Joel fixed his window. We were sitting eating dinner as was our usual Monday night custom and the phone rang. I jumped up amid laughter and answered the phone.

'Hello, can I speak to a Miss Philippa Hanna please?' said an official, yet very broad Yorkshire drawl, on the other end.

'That's me.'

'Oh, hello. I'm calling with regards to a bag reported stolen last week.' My heart began to race.

'Yes that's right, it was stolen from my boyfriend's car.'

'Ah, well you know you should never leave things on display.'

'Well, I know, I just thought it wouldn't be a problem in Ecclesall. I guess there's crime everywhere though.'

'Can you just describe that bag for us again please?'

'Erm yes, it was a large, black record bag with padded panels. It had a make-up bag and a denim purse in it, as well as some keys with a wooden-cow key ring. The legs are broken though.'

'Yes, I'm pleased to say that it has been found.'

I couldn't believe my left ear.

'Really? With the stuff?'

'Was there any money in the purse Miss Hanna?'

I felt a little embarrassed.

'Err, no not really. Maybe a few coins.'

'Right, well it looks like everything's still there then. It's a bit muddy and it looks like he's gone through your purse but everything you've described is still intact.'

I ended the call and shared the good news with my housemates. We got in the car and went down to the station to collect it. Everything was there: my cards, keys and make-up. I could see that he'd tried to go through the purse and found nothing. He hadn't taken my Bible either.

'So where did you find it then?' I asked the policeman, relieved beyond measure.

'Well, just up the road from the church. It had been tossed over a stone wall into some bushes. He probably had a quick look for some cash or a phone and then scarpered when he didn't find any.' I sighed. I was so fortunate to have pocketed my phone on the journey that morning.

I just couldn't believe someone would go to the trouble of breaking a window only to toss the bag over a wall without even taking any of the contents. It didn't make sense. I signed some paperwork and went home.

The next morning something strange happened. I had another phone call from the police.

'Morning Miss Hanna it's PC something-or-other. I wouldn't mind having another little chat with you if you don't mind. Could I call round please?' I was terrified!

'Of course,' I answered, racking my brain for any crimes I may have unwittingly committed in the last twenty-four hours. What if they'd found something planted in my bag and not told me?

The officer sat at my table and began his strange kind of questioning.

'We've actually got someone for this robbery,' he began. 'Now we've been after this chap for some time. But he told us something very unusual about your bag.' My pulse was racing by now. What was going on here?

'Now, he threw it over a wall, which is not unusual in an opportunistic robbery like that, but he mentioned some kind of strange leaflet he'd found in your bag.' My mind raced.

'Some kind of Satanic document.' I couldn't quite process what the policeman was saying. What was he accusing me of?

'Satanic? I'm a Christian. My Bible was in my bag! I can't think what he'd be talking about.' My brain was doing overtime. I was genuinely confused.

The officer elaborated, 'Well, the guy is saying that he was so freaked out by this leaflet that he tossed your bag and legged it.' He continued, 'He said something about an organization that was trying to kill Jesus. It said, "But they couldn't get rid of Jesus" or something like that.' Suddenly the penny dropped.

'Oh my goodness. That's not a Satanic thing! That's an evangelical leaflet that a Christian gave me in town. It's about how Jesus was crucified but he rose again.'

The officer was looking a little confused. Then I remembered something. I raced to my noticeboard upstairs and to my relief found one there. It was an exact copy of the leaflet eager Cedric the street-preacher had given me on more than one occasion.

'Here it is, this is exactly the same as the one in my bag.' I handed the tract over.

'The man they couldn't get rid of,' it said on the cover. The officer flicked through and chuckled to himself.

'So he saw this and thought it was something scary. How ironic.'

The officer left taking the leaflet with him. I never heard another word about it.

I couldn't believe the power that the mention of Jesus had. It felt like I'd been protected and against all odds (and my own stupidity). I had managed to get all my things back and the thief had been caught. I just hoped the officer had a chance to explain what the leaflet was really about.

CAR CRASH

JOEL FIXED his passenger door window without too much of a fuss and the car was back to normal. Things were going pretty well between us. The days were bringing us closer and it was wonderful to experience a relationship that wasn't based solely on the physical. I felt so safe. So, I really wasn't expecting what happened one evening.

I had my overnight bag packed again, but this time it would remain at my side. We were heading to Joel's parents' house for the evening. We were quite excited as the table was set for a fancy family dinner.

Joel's folks lived out in Rotherham and we soon found ourselves on the home stretch of the drive. As was customary, we had music on and I was singing along jovially. Joel was his usual, mellow self, driving carefully and keeping his mind on the road.

As we hit the last main road of the journey we approached a large country pub called The Red Lion. The grand inn stands a little back from the roadside, and drivers have to pause in the right-hand lane of the dual carriageway in order to turn into the car park.

We'd been to The Red Lion a couple of times. It was a typical Yorkshire pub with wooden-spoon table numbers and candles in wine-bottles. At this stretch of road we found ourselves behind a rather large lorry. The car in front was overtaking it.

Joel, now conscious of the time, saw no reason not to do the same. He pulled out into the right-hand lane and put his foot to the floor. It's hard to explain what I felt at that moment, but it was definitely 'unsafe'. Joel is a careful, steady driver and I have never felt anything other than secure in his car. But just then, I had a terrible feeling that something was wrong. The music played out confidently as the situation unravelled before us.

As the car in front passed the lorry, we faced a horrible realization: a car had stopped at the turn-in for the pub. It was stationary with the indicator on. Joel's reactions kicked in and he slammed on the brakes, but everything in me knew that there wasn't enough time. We were heading for a collision.

There was a strange moment of silence after the accident. I knew without looking that the blood had drained from our faces. The music had stopped as the car cut out, but it began booming again within seconds. It was hard to believe how different the atmosphere had been before that last chorus. I quickly looked down to check I was still all there. Not a bruise or scratch.

'Are you OK?' I asked Joel in a panic.

'Yeah I'm fine,' he said, before coming to his senses. 'Crap, crap, crap!' he posh-cussed while hopping out of the car to assess the damage and check on the other driver.

The other driver emerged unharmed from his car in a mild state of shock. The back of his sturdy vehicle looked to be in one piece. Perhaps it hadn't been so bad? Suddenly it dawned on me that we were still in the middle of the road. I jumped out of the car and onto the grass verge for safety. Joel chatted to the other driver and then called his dad.

Having witnessed the crash, another driver had stopped, and then another. They helped us push Joel's car out of the road and onto the embankment. When I saw the front of the car, I realized how fortunate we'd been; it was completely crushed. The loud crunch of the metal rang through my mind. There's no sound quite like it. I wondered if I'd be in pain when the shock wore off, and felt across my chest where the seat belt had saved me. But there wasn't even a bruise or an ache.

Joel's dad broke away from the dinner party, which by now was in full swing, and came to the rescue. He called the police and brought Joel and I home. I allowed Joel the time to chat to his dad alone before I joined them. I knew he was upset with himself, and shocked as well. But we were alright.

Once at the party, we sat down to dinner like nothing had happened and retold the tale to moans of sympathy. Later that evening we reflected that we were very fortunate. But we faced the reality that there was no longer a car for Joel to drive around in.

'I just can't stop thinking that, "In all things God works for the good of those who love him, who are called according to his purpose"' (Romans 8:28), said Joel's dad Phil. 'There has to be some good in this somehow.'

We hoped he was right. In the meantime we were just glad to be safe. It was such a testament to the seatbelt, as well as to God's goodness. A few weeks later Joel received the news that with the insurance payout plus a little extra he'd be able to get a much better car. I'm not suggesting that God caused this to happen, but it did confirm Phil's quote from Scripture that God can find a way of bringing something positive from something negative. And so the story continues . . .

A Word in Season

I STEPPED into church that night feeling heavy. It had been almost six months since I'd asked God to help me sort my life out. I'd got a job and had begun to settle in Sheffield. But a dull fatigue was sweeping over me. Where was my breakthrough? Surely God didn't bring me all the way to Sheffield simply to work in a bar? On the one hand I felt so selfish. He was doing so much in me – the songs were rolling out, my debts were finally under control, my relationships were healing and I was beginning to feel human again. But on the other hand, I was having trouble understanding this great 'plan' of his. I still felt like a lamp hidden under a bowl.

That evening Andy Rushworth spoke on something relating to our purpose in God. The message prickled my skin. My heart was hardening a little. Prayer didn't seem to be working. Just as the meeting was closing, an opportunity came to go to the front for prayer.

Andy's wife Sharon was praying for people at the front. At church I'd become known for my enthusiasm and confidence. I felt slightly awkward appearing in the prayer line, feeling downcast and desperate. But my legs took me.

As I stood there, listening to the band and waiting for prayer, I tried to soak in reassurance from God. But a wall of unbelief was building. I was willing to give my life and my dreams to God and to be his servant. But I couldn't ignore the longing in my heart to do more.

As Sharon reached me, something happened. She touched my shoulder and I felt myself melting as she spoke.

'God knows what he's doing Philippa. He didn't give you those visions and dreams for no reason. He didn't put those gifts in you for no reason. He has a plan.' By the time she'd uttered those first words I was breaking. I was choking on months' worth of tears. They were tears of frustration, disappointment and anxiety.

I experienced God's reassurance through Sharon that night. She spoke straight into my concern. I held tight to those words and prepared myself to serve All Bar One faithfully until such a time as God might move me out from that place.

TALKING TO STRANGERS

I GREW to love my life in Sheffield. It wasn't easy waitressing full-time. I developed a deep respect for those who work in hospitality. Sometimes my feet felt like they were spontaneously combusting. And then there was the stress of making mistakes. On a busy lunch hour when throngs of suits would file in and expect a three-course lunch in an hour, it was well and truly all hands on deck.

I'll never forget taking six hot, loaded burgers out to a table of solicitors in three-piece suits, only to realize that their starters were still waiting in the kitchen.

But I was getting good at the job. My tips were going up. It was an incredible feeling being rewarded for my hard work and friendliness right there on the spot. My relationships at work were improving as well. Lee, the straight-talking Sheffield chap with a typically gritty chef's vocabulary, was becoming a friend. There was something about the way he got straight to the point that I connected with. He always wanted to talk about my new faith. He couldn't believe that I was waiting for marriage to sleep with Joel. The staff talked about it regularly in the kitchen. Despite the jibes I sensed a respect about my lifestyle choice.

The other bonus about working at All Bar One was the regulars. There were several who made a big impression on me, including a harmless and pleasant, yet arguably bonkers, regular who talked to her own earrings.

'I'm a secret agent,' she once told me.

I met many a special person over a tapas bundle and mid-afternoon tipple. One particular morning it wasn't a customer who chatted to me. In fact, I hadn't even got through the glass doors.

The bus journey to work took about twenty minutes each morning. I always used the time to get some more of the Bible into my system. This particular morning the bus was quite crowded, so I had to sit facing backwards in a four-seat section.

I was deeply engrossed in reading when I heard a voice say, 'I used to read that thing you know.' I looked up to see a guy in his late twenties with thick, curly hair. He was wearing a tracksuit.

'Are you one of them Christians then?' he asked.

'Yep,' I said smiling.

'What, do you go to church 'n' that?'

'Yeah, do you?' I replied.

'Nah, not me love. I did used to believe actually but not now. I've seen some bad things love. No, there's no place for someone like me in church.' This had to be a God appointment.

'That's the thing though.' I said. 'Jesus accepts everyone.' I sounded like a bona fide God-botherer. I tried to make my accent a little thicker so as not to sound like a nun.

'Well,' he said with raised eyebrows, 'if you knew what I was on my way to do you wouldn't say that.' What had I got myself into? There was a pause.

'I don't know what you're on your way to do but . . .' I was searching for the words. 'You said you used to believe.

Well, maybe God has put me opposite you this morning for a reason. To tell you not to do anything you'll regret.' It was bizarre, the stuff of stories. But here we were.

He gazed out of the window, hunched forward with his hands clasped. He looked as though he was watching the future – seeing himself in action. He was almost licking his lips.

'Yeah, maybe you're right love. But, you know – some things need sorting out. Some things you just can't do nothing about. Especially when it's family.' I was getting the picture.

'Has someone hurt your family?'

'My sister. This guy deserves everything he gets. What if it was your family?' He seemed calm, yet he was eerily focused on his plan.

'It is so hard with family.' I wasn't going to deny that. Sometimes revenge seems right. I searched my brain for anything that might leave an impression.

'But I guess you have to leave it in God's hands. I would just believe that God was going to sort it out. And also, if something kicks off and you get hurt your family will be devastated.' It was true. And I knew the words hadn't really come from me.

We reached town and got up to get off the bus. He stuck a cap on as we hit the drizzly street.

'Well preacher-girl. Thanks for the chat. Maybe I'll behave myself after all,' he said, smiling as he began to walk down Fargate.

I continued to the bar. I don't know what he had planned to do. I would never know if he took my advice. But I did know this – that was no ordinary bus ride in the rain.

CHRISTMAS MIRACLE

DECEMBER 2005 came around fast. Club shows had now petered out so I'd been trying to pick up extra shifts at the bar. Thanks to the usual turnover of student part-timers, extra shifts had become available. In fact I was more full-time than ever.

The bar was warm and cosy around Christmastime. Frost softened the angular windows and the scent of cinnamon mulled wine spiced the air. Being part of a chain meant that the bar was subject to change at any moment. Some mornings we would arrive to a completely rearranged bar and see workmen clearing up from their all-nighter in time for breakfast. At Christmas it was more like Elves had invaded during the night leaving baubles and tinsel in their wake. A large deep-green fir tree stood proudly in the front window, decked with all shades of purple and gold. The holiday spirit made work more relaxed.

But Christmas is expensive in the city. The usual shopping for presents for family and friends is hard on minimum wage. To be quite frank, my bank account had never looked sadder. It's not a great feeling – facing the season of peace and goodwill without the cash to enjoy the staff night out or the January sales. The rent still needed to be paid in January, and hours always decreased after Christmas.

It was 23 December. I remember the date because it was my final shift – all that stood between me and two days off.

It had been a crazy season. The mood was lighter, but the bar was also busier. Old friends were meeting for annual catch-ups. Spare seats accommodated piles of shopping. Work-dos took up our long tables.

At 11 a.m. guests were arriving thick and fast. Orders for seasonal tapas dishes and liqueur coffees were coming in one after the other. A group of work colleagues arrived and sat down. They hit the most expensive champagne straight away and made their way through it almost as fast as we could chill extra bottles. They left two hours later leaving a £20 tip on the silver tray! These blessings were definitely counted.

Christmas Eve came, and we went to the carol service at Joel's church. It was quaint and uplifting. Candles surrounded the room and the tree was lit up softly in the corner. When the offering basket came around, I found my heart twitching. Something in me said: 'put the £20 in.' It was my last £20.

There's a lot that I could say about what different denominations encourage and teach about giving. But because that leaves so much room for debate, I want to steer clear of the technical details. But, there is a certain promise to reward what's given in faith: 'You must each decide in your heart how much to give. And don't give reluctantly or in response to pressure. For God loves a person who gives cheerfully' (2 Corinthians 9:7 NLT).

Before I could miss the basket, I whipped out the £20 note and threw it in. I won't lie; it was with a little hesitation. But in my heart I felt that it was the right thing to do.

Christmas Day came and went. On Boxing Day I was back to work at the bar. Far from the heaving hustle and bustle of two days back, all was still in All Bar One. The customers comprised of an elderly gentleman with a winter hat and walking stick, and a couple clearly in need of respite from their relatives. It was what you might call 'dead' and it was a welcome peace. It didn't bode well for tips though. How quickly the abundant abandon of December becomes the penny-pinching plight of January.

'Pay-slips are up there,' mentioned Mark as he made his way through to the kitchen. In the walkway to the kitchen was the small staff cubbyhole. We kept our keys and loose change in there between shifts. The usual end-of-week bundle sat by the ashtrays. I pulled off the elastic band and flicked through for my name. I absent-mindedly ripped it open.

Expecting to see the usual £90.01 plus £20.45 tip, I almost fell over. There was in excess of £500.00! It couldn't be right, could it? Not daring to believe I'd seen right, I took a sip of lime and soda and looked again.

I hadn't realized, but I'd been paying emergency tax since my first day at All Bar One. My tax code had finally been rectified. It was a Christmas courtesy of HMRC. I bounced around the bar sharing the good news with my colleagues.

A Sound Investment

MY EYES creaked open like an old chest. The alarm tone bubbled around my tiny green room, growing louder with each moment. My throat ground against itself as I swallowed. The stale residue of second-hand smoke coated my throat from my long shift at the bar the previous day. The blind in my room was half down as usual (it had stuck one day and I decided to roll with it). The day outside was grey, rainy and cold.

I looked at the clock. It read 9 a.m. Andy had booked in a practice with the boys. I pictured the cold church with its Saturday frost, long before the Sunday thaw that brings people, prayers and coffee. I imagined singing through the thick fog in my throat. I was still new to band rehearsals. Before the band, I'd always conquered my musical demons in private. I still felt pressure to impress, dumbfounded that they wanted to play my songs.

It was so good of Andy to have taken me on in this way. He believed in me, that much was clear. But I was flagging in my new life, working full-time and filling weekends with church activities. The bed swallowed my heavy body as I reached for the phone.

'Andy, I can't do the practice this morning. I'm just not feeling up to it,' I began. Quickly the conversation became strained. Then it elevated.

'Look, to be honest Philippa, I don't want to work with someone who's not dedicated.' The words cut right through me. He was frustrated. The only way I knew how to respond was to be defensive.

I had been doing better up to that point – good was winning over bad. In that moment I stopped myself from being downright abusive. There was no swearing and shouting. My progress was clear. But something else was clear too: Andy was focused, driven and uncompromising. He was fed up of trying to spoon-feed me a future. He wanted the best from me, but I was knackered. The conversation ended badly; we were both angry and upset.

Over the following few days I felt defeated. Above all, I was deeply disappointed with myself.

I confided in Joel, 'I'm not sure whether I should give up on all this. I desperately want to do something with my music, but it doesn't seem to be happening. I feel like I'm wasting my time.'

Joel listened gently, adding nothing but absorbing my tears with his shirt.

That Sunday I saw Andy. He hugged me and apologized. He promised not to abandon the band, but it was decided that I needed more time.

One morning a week or so later I began to pick up the pieces. I called the boys and suggested we meet up and jam again. Pretty soon I was there with my guitar – playing with the band. Drums and bass surrounded the picking and strumming. Without Andy, I felt a bit more free to learn and make mistakes.

In those rehearsals, the Dawson brothers and I developed a true connection. Once again I had something to look forward to. We worked on some new material and had a half-decent set.

One song really stood out. It was called 'Higher' and it was a landmark for me. It was honest and positive. I was really beginning to bond with the old six-string by now; I wasn't so shy of her anymore. As practices went on, I felt more and more disappointed not to be working with Andy. I couldn't help thinking that we might be recording material by now, something that was desperately close to my heart. I longed so deeply to make an album of my own – filled with songs that documented this journey.

The bar was comfortably busy the afternoon barman Tom propositioned me – not in any seedy way, I hasten to add. Tom was a music student studying at Sheffield University. He was clever and ever so slightly cocky. We bonded over music, something that we obviously shared a genuine passion for. That passion made dull Monday afternoons become colourful comparisons of taste, air-blogs of favourite all-time acts and dreams for the future.

'Philippa, I was wondering if you could help me out with something,' Tom started, 'Might you and your band be available to record something with me for uni? I have to engineer a session and submit two separate recordings.' My face must have doubled in brightness, a grin from ear to ear.

'Totally – that would be amazing,' I replied. I was so flattered to be approached in this way – as a musician with a band and original material.

Shortly after, the boys and I joined Tom for the session. In the cosy university studio we recorded two new songs.

One was a track called 'Crazy Days', and the aforementioned 'Higher'. After laying down drums, bass and acoustic, Tim and Pete left and I braced myself to begin the vocals.

It was a moment I won't forget. Of course I'd done vocals before – in the lush Steelworks vocal booth steeped in its warm hit-factory haze, and a thousand times in my own bedroom workspace. But this was different. I did three takes. Number three was the one we kept. As my nerves subsided, they made way for something more powerful – a desire for Tom to hear my heart. With every note my heart began to speak, 'Tom, this is my story. It's true – God has set me free.'

Weeks later, I was with Andy. I guess we were preparing worship or heading to the warm confines of the Prince of Wales pub (the unofficial post-church venue). I played him the demos. Andy is a man of measured response. He can be quite the entertainer and is certainly not a bore. But when it comes to his work, he doesn't overreact. On this occasion, he was visibly excited. He loved the material and the band sounded great, but it wasn't really the songs that did it. It was the fact I'd got my act together. It was the sign he'd been waiting for. In his endearingly cagey way, he sort of suggested we make an album.

We'll have to cut the scene there, because at this point my brain winds swiftly forward to a cold afternoon at the Baker residence. Andy's folks had always been kind to me on my visits to Sheffield. Groups of us would often wind up there post-Anvil for teas and TV. This afternoon they were hovering away gently in respective housekeeping tasks.

Andy and I are in the office. The pen is in my hand and I'm signing a piece of paper. It's a contract between me and Andy

Baker. He is putting £3,000 of his own money into an album fund. He's about to produce my first album: *Watching Me*.

Over the weeks that followed, we chipped away at material. The first playbacks blew me away. The album started to come together. The songs were well recorded and they sounded clean and full. Vocals were a challenge. I was still struggling with the tobacco-ridden air in the bar. Some of the recording sessions were hard work, but I prayed that somehow my ability would surface in the sound.

Good Pennies

ANDY WASTED no time planning the album release. Every week we'd meet and plan our next moves. I continued working at the bar. One shift I started chatting to a bearded stranger.

He was a friendly Yorkshireman wearing a black bomber-jacket and well-worn jeans. He was in the pub for an early Friday pint. I guess it must have been quiet because we had quite a conversation.

'You're a happy waitress,' he chirped, after I responded to a handful of his banter offerings. 'It makes a lovely change.'

I said what I always used to say when someone commented on my chipper mood. 'I have every reason to be happy,' I said, grinning.

'Yeah, why's that?' he inquired with a wry smile.

'I'm a Christian. I became a Christian a couple of years ago and it's changed my life.' He was a little thrown by this, but still game for the conversation. He wasn't hardened to faith, but fired challenging questions my way nonetheless.

As he left, I picked up a couple of pounds change he'd left me on the bar. He had walked out with a smile on his face, and as I cleaned the coffee machine, I had a smile on mine.

At that time I was involved in something called The Rockalates tour. The theme was chocolate because the band I was supporting was Belgian. A good friend, William Bode, had arranged the tour. A music enthusiast and very evangelistic Christian, William had first spotted me supporting The Gentlemen at one of their many sold-out gigs at Sheffield's live music venue, The Plug.

I remember the gig well. I'd worn a sparkly, hot-pink, sequinned shrug over a T-shirt with a denim skirt. I was only a couple of gigs into working with the band and playing the guitar. The place had been packed. I did what I went to do, played my songs and talked about this strange event that seemed to be changing everything. As I looked across the packed room, soaking up the warmth I was ever more convinced – God was in this.

Being a Christian, William made a beeline for me after the gig. He asked if I'd like to support a band on a short UK tour. I began to bounce up and down with excitement, saying, 'Yes, yes, yes!' in response. He gave me his card and we took it from there.

Tonight was the second night of the tour. We were playing a local bar. It wasn't really made for a live band, truth be known. It was a great venue, but we were battling against a DJ throughout the whole set. Still, we played our best. I pulled 'The Summer of '69' and played till my fingers bled (that's a Bryan Adams reference for any of you confused at this point). I remember the feeling of hot liquid sliding down my nails and splattering onto the pale guitar body. It wasn't the first time and it wouldn't be the last.

Surprisingly though, the set went well. As I moved over to the CD area to chat to people, a chap approached me.

'Well, this is just spooky,' he said. As my eyes focused, I realized who the familiar chap was – it was Mr Bomber-jacket from the bar. We chatted briefly about coincidence versus design and, although he was still ready to make a case in defence, he was struggling to contest this one. It turned out that William and his wife Lyssa had been chatting to him for some time. He was a colleague.

PREPARE TO LAUNCH

MY TWO worst fears were finding no support for my music and not being able to perform it live. I was still at the mercy of stage fright. Andy Baker made me face both fears in one night. He wanted me to do an album launch.

All Saints Church was the venue. The double-edged sword was its size. It was big enough to hold 400 people at least. It could look very empty if numbers were poor.

I was surprised to find that people wanted to help organize the event. The great youth guys at The Anvil stepped up to run tuck shops and cart gear around. A dozen people volunteered.

The morning of the launch arrived. It was an early start. At 8 a.m. I awoke to another dread: a troublesome cough. The burn was definitely there. It was the worst-case scenario for me, the ultimate undermining of my confidence for the evening. Despite this, we got to work. We set up merchandise, spent hours practising and soundchecking.

Then the craziest thing happened. A whole team of ladies turned up with a van full of goodies. They began decking out the huge space with fresh flowers and fruit.

'Did you know about this Andy?' I asked, perplexed at the implications. What was all this?

'Yeah,' he responded thoughtfully, 'I think it's the harvest festival service tomorrow.'

My eyes swept around the busy church. There were people everywhere, all arranging wheat sheaves and fruit. Banners were being hung and candles replaced.

Right at that moment, a tiny seed of faith formed in my chest, like the smallest speck of gold dust in a muddy stream. It was as though the decorations were a sign. It was like someone, somewhere had already been planning this event. It was a celebration of life and restoration. It was as if God got there before us and had begun his plans. This was a special occasion that God had already organized – like a wedding – a public declaration of love and a new beginning.

I looked at the vast empty room. Despite all my fears, I was certain of one thing – I wanted it to be a powerful evening that would touch people's hearts.

Steph helped me to get ready in the vestry behind the platform. As I put on my make-up I peered into the slowly filling room. It really was filling up. The first half was torture as I listened in on the support acts. They were all brilliant. Becky Higg, a writer with a gentle, brilliant voice, opened up acoustically. She drew the crowd in beautifully. I peeped out. The room was full. It was a potent yet terrifying feeling. They were there for me, yay; they were there for me, eek.

Finally, it was time for the set to begin. I'd dosed up on cough medicine and flu tablets. Roo began playing. The music began to build, and finally it was time to step onto the stage. I walked out to warm applause, my heart pounding and my mouth dry. I began to sing.

'Jesus, we pray, let your holiness bring a song of salvation,' I sang. As the words left my mouth, flowing out toward the back walls of the church, my cough seemed non-existent. I only wanted to worship God and seize this moment for him. If this was the last gig I'd ever play, if no one ever turned out to hear me sing again, I wanted to sing for my life.

Just then, my friends from work filtered in gingerly. My heart quickened again. They were here *in church* to hear my story. After the show they came to buy CDs. The group was positive and upbeat. As the night drew to a close, I drifted to cloud nine. Fatigue hit my bones from the adrenaline and the flu and I collapsed in a euphoric haze in the car. It had all been a success.

At Joel's house that night we shared a bottle of champagne that had been given to me that night as a congratulations present.

'I actually got quite emotional watching you sing,' he said.

'Really? Why?'

'Well, you know, it's not long since you were wondering if you should give up. Then there you were on stage giving your testimony and launching your first album.'

'Yeah,' I said, grateful for the support. As we sat in Phil and Yvonne's lounge with glasses of champagne in hand and watching TV, I felt so peaceful.

The launch was a milestone. It was everything a launch should be. I was slowly finding my feet in this new world. I loved to tell this story.

Radio Coma

THE ALL BAR ONE manager Andy, was a star during this time. I remember him perching at the high table by the bar, scribbling away thanklessly at the rota.

'My least favourite job,' he'd say, the closest he'd ever get to complaining. The rota was a tough job. Most employees were students who were forever swapping shifts and needing time off. Thank God for Alex Plant's shift-hoarding ways. He was usually willing to pick up the slack, loving the challenge and the extra tips. I still loved the bar. By now it was a home from home.

One morning while I was putting bags in bins and chopping fruit ready for bar service, Andy breezed up from the cellar. He was his usual mellow self. In his line-cleaning clothes he just looked like a young lad really.

'You're looking very nice today Phil,' he said. He had a sweet habit of shortening everyone's name.

'Thanks Andy!' I said, blushing a little. For two years I'd bought all my clothes from charity shops, with the odd vintage bargain thrown into the mix. I'd been saving every penny to pay off my debts. That week I'd treated myself to some new leggings and a top as I was about to start my first tour – small gigs around the country, whatever we could find. I still couldn't quite believe what was happening.

'Yeah,' he said, hand behind his neck. 'I don't think we'll be having Philippa around here much longer.'

'Oh,' I said, 'I'm not sure about that.'

'Yeah, you'll be away after this tour. Don't think we'll be seeing much of you after that.' I appreciated the vote of confidence.

'Aw,' I said, feeling a little sad, though sparkling beneath with excitement at the prospect.

'No, it's great! I'm happy for you. You deserve it. You'll be missed.' Andy was a special boss. He was someone I looked forward to working with and was sad to say goodbye to.

Amy was also someone I was close to. She was a complex character. Her passion for hospitality made her quick and practical. She always had enough energy. She was keen to be manager at some stage, and at that time she was a supervisor.

But there was more to Amy than met the eye. We had some real moments. She was also pretty gorgeous and had done some modelling pre-bar.

One day, a curious chap came in. He was wearing a long, black woollen coat and curls were licking out from beneath a flat cap. He had an eerie journalist's presence. I was both drawn to, and afraid of him. Amy ran over and swung her arms round him like an excited kid.

'That's Stevlor,' she said after he left. 'I did some modelling for his magazine. You should have a word with him about your music.' My heart filled with dread. He didn't look the sort to favour Christian music. This would be the album's first real encounter with the mainstream press. I feared the worst: 'Bible-bashing rubbish', 'Lame and irrelevant.' Poor headlines and reviews flooded the dark part of my imagination.

The next time Stevlor came in he had a record bag with him. We started chatting as I cleared his glasses and he reached for the bag.

'This is my magazine,' he said, pulling out an edgy-looking music mag. On the front was a slightly dark picture – a skinny, naked female with various pieces of music equipment covering her anatomy. The title read *Radio Coma* and the strapline said *The heroin not the aspirin*. My stomach churned. This was certainly not the *Joy* magazine.

'I'd love to give your stuff a review.' I wasn't sure. It seemed like a massive gamble. I flicked to music reviews spread across the centre page. One leapt out at me as being particularly cruel. My heart began to flutter and my mouth went dry.

'Just hold on a sec, I'll be back in a minute,' I said, before racing downstairs to the staffroom. I frantically punched in the door code. I rifled into my bag and pulled out a copy of *Watching Me*. I always carried a couple of copies as Andy had taught me – it's a musician's best business card.

'Here you go.' I winced, holding out the jewel case, my heart seeping out of the plastic sides. 'Please be kind.' He gave me a sly smile, slightly raising one jet-black eyebrow and disappeared through the heavy glass doors.

'Former slapper releases hypocritical album,' screamed the headline. I sat bolt upright in bed, my brow damp with fear. Phew, it was just a dream. Actually it was a vivid nightmare. Was it a sign? It was so real, the kind that stays with you into the afternoon.

It may seem irrelevant or insignificant to you at this point dear reader, but I assure you this was significant. To me it felt like looking down the barrel of a gun.

One morning at work Amy mentioned the magazine, 'Oh, I think it's out you know. It should definitely be out by now.' My heart flew into my mouth.

'What, really? Oh my goodness, I'm so nervous.'

'Why?' she screeched. 'I'm sure he wouldn't give you a bad review. Your songs are lovely.'

'Yeah, I hope so. Where would I find a copy?' She paused mid bar-wipe.

'The Frog and Parrot. I think they stock it in there. Go out on your break if you like and get a copy.' My heart stayed firmly between my teeth.

At break time, I walked up the high street to the Frog and Parrot. It was a crusty, characterful bar at the time and a regular host for local band gigs and open mics. There was usually a guy from a band behind the bar.

I looked around but couldn't see the mag anywhere.

''Scuse me,' I said to the hairy boy behind the taps. 'You don't happen to have a copy of *Coma* do you? I have a review in there,' I said nervously. He looked at me.

'Oh yeah, I've seen that,' he said, recognizing my picture. He called to the tattooed girl at the other end of the bar.

'Have we got that copy of *Coma* left?' The girl hopped up and came back with the magazine. He began flicking though, found the review section and tossed it towards me.

'It's pretty good.'

My eyes flicked from word to word. I hardly dared to read it – maybe I wouldn't have, had the barman not reassured me.

I had teeth pulled once aged six and waiting for a dentist to stick some pliers in my mouth wasn't as bad as this.

I started to read, one sentence at a time. As the words trickled through my fear filter I realized the review was good. No, it wasn't just good – it was a *glowing* review. I was thunderstruck. Scanning over the other reviews on the page, the language was markedly different. To my total surprise, there was no mockery or jibing. Whoever had listened to the album had obviously liked it, in spite of the gushy, happy-clappiness.

It said:

PHILIPPA HANNA Watching Me *(Resound Media)*

Now historically, songs about how God has transformed your life usually only get aired via Stars On Sunday, *Monday morning assembly or when it's baby Jesus time. They are also usually pretty bland and unimaginative and rarely bear any semblance to popular modern music structure, with throwaway tunes and constant banging-on about their Saviour. Philippa Hanna is a little more off-centre. Though she celebrates her evangelism these songs ain't kicking you hard with religion and, had I not already mentioned the Christian aspect, on hearing these tunes you'd accept them as a body of work that would give Alanis and co a good run and not feel you'd been brow-beaten onto the prayer stool. There's a lot of groove coated bluesy pop here, a little countrified with vocals sweeter than Pooh Bear's whiskers after a night in the honey jar. If you like your tunes mellow with a slight stick of dynamite this is the album for you.*

I skipped out from the bar on cloud nine, relieved and amazed. The good review was so unlikely that it felt like a miracle. I also realized that sometimes your heart can fill with dread, and it's not at all from God.

PART 4
ON WITH THE JOURNEY

ACID TEST

So, WE'VE been talking about miracles. I realize that some of these events and occurrences may not be worthy of Vatican approval. My hope is that you'll see every event as another breadcrumb that would lead me out of darkness and into a new world. My hope is that each piece of the puzzle shows you a picture of how God can intervene in a life 'gone wrong' and turn it into something special: a life worth getting out of bed for each day. The following story is more like the other kind of miracle.

This incident took place on a missions' trip. A special speaker came to Sheffield Christian Life Centre. His name was LaVere Soper and he was a longstanding friend of Joel's dad. LaVere had everything you'd hope a visiting speaker would have: authority, experience and a faith that was contagious. He spent most of the year travelling around the many churches that he'd helped plant and was now overseeing. He'd initiated dozens of ministries worldwide. His life was all about living for something more. He was living out faith in an inspiring and undeniable way. He was also known for his ministry of healing.

Now, I know this area is touchy for many, as reports of manipulative capitalist charlatans are rife. Footage of healing rallies where poor people are encouraged to give generously to offerings have given the term 'healing ministry' some pretty bad press. When I'd flicked over to religious programming on cable TV, I'd shaken my head as cynically as the next agnostic and been quick to jump on a soapbox about money-greedy televangelists.

But after I became a part of the church it didn't take me long to learn that a belief in God as a healer was integral to the Christian faith. In the New Testament healing was a hallmark of Jesus' ministry. The Bible says that after Jesus ascended into heaven the disciples were filled with the Holy Spirit. At that moment, they were given power and authority to heal the sick, just as Jesus did.

So, I now understood the church's view – God could still perform all manner of miracles *through* ordinary people who'd been filled with the Spirit. Of course, in today's cynical world this is a controversial claim, which leaves us vulnerable to all kind of mockery and persecution. But it's very hard to argue with a case of someone's healed body. I was about to see some of this stuff first-hand.

LaVere gathered the youth together to invite us on a missions' trip to Hungary. I was very new to the Sheffield Christian Life Centre and wasn't actively involved in any ministry there.

'This is going to be a huge step for you in your faith,' said LaVere with conviction. 'I encourage you to make this commitment if you want to grow in your walk with God.'

As I heard those words something within me, I guess you could say it was the Holy Spirit, prompted me to put my name down. So I did.

It was going to be remarkably cheap – just a couple of hundred pounds each for the week. Flights to Hungary were pennies and we would be staying in a hostel. Our 'mission' was to spend time with people in a church and work with the youth. We were going to run workshops and playtimes with the younger ones (through an interpreter which scared me witless). We were also going to be serving physically in the renovation of a building. The church we would be visiting was building a centre to train and educate members of a large Gypsy community. It was all pretty scary stuff but I felt a warmth about going. Now all I'd have to do was raise the cash.

Over the weeks that followed, I saved my tips in a jar for the trip. I had the agreed amount of cash ready and put it in an envelope. I delivered it proudly one Sunday to be met with something of a bombshell.

'OK, it turned out it's going to be a little bit more than that,' Luke (who was involved with running the trip) said, with his usual wry smile. My jaw dropped. Phil reassured me afterwards. This was what mission was all about – leaning on God for your needs and seeing his power as you lay down your life to serve others.

With one week to go I was praying hard. I had nothing in the bank to spare and it was only days until the trip. At this point I really saw God's provision. It started with a generous morning-coffee sipper who left a £5 tip. 'Really? For a £3 bill?' I thought. But there was no mistake. There it was. And it just kept going. A barrister on his lunch break left £20. Table after table left gold coins instead of silver, notes instead of coins. It felt as if it wasn't going to end.

I'd told my colleagues about the trip and my need to raise more money, so this miraculous provision was working well for my witness in the kitchen.

The usual kitchen banter continued about my faith. They'd tease me in good humour about the sex-before-marriage stuff and various other things. But I always kept them in the loop about what I was doing and what I was believing God for. I think they enjoyed the entertainment. During a busy Friday night shift, I shared with the boss that I was fasting. It wasn't sensible to fast on a Friday night as it was so busy. But my energy was boundless; I zipped around the place like I'd downed some kind of protein shake. I didn't bother with a break (there was no food to look forward to after all). That shift earned me £60 in tips. It all went into the pot.

When the moment came to pay Luke the cash was there – every penny. Now at this point you might ask, why? Why should God supply an airfare and not the other financial needs of the planet? This is a question I once asked and I began to see the answer over time. There's always a reason with God. He doesn't do things 'just 'cos'. He has a purpose for every healing, every provision and every manifestation of his presence. That purpose is to increase our faith and reveal his power, so that we might go forward and share what he's done.

I felt a little out of sorts once we arrived in Hungary. The food was different, the language was incomprehensible and we had a gruelling week of service tasks to perform. It seemed a little mad to have chosen this. That's when LaVere announced we'd be meeting every morning at dawn to pray and read the Bible. I wasn't fond of this news. I've never been a morning person and the week was looking tiring already. I bit my tongue and hoped for the best.

The first morning was interesting. I yawned my way up to the meeting place and was surprised to be served a beautiful

Hungarian breakfast. As we chatted and sipped away on our coffees LaVere began to pray and to teach us. I was gripped. His words were filled with warmth and authority. I soaked them in, suddenly realizing that there was more to this trip than I'd expected.

We went from breakfast to the Gypsy training centre. It certainly needed some TLC. In a flash our host appeared with protective clothing, massive vats of paint stripper and a box of tools.

'This morning's task is to strip all the paint off the window sills.' I looked around. There were lots of windowsills. And a lot of paint on those windowsills.

'Please be very careful as this substance is very strong and should not make contact with skin. Wear the protective overalls,' our host continued. We stared at the pile of clothes and agreed in some kind of feigned excitement.

Once changed we looked like a mob of homicidal Tweenies – we were dressed head-to-toe in baggy, white onesies, masks and goggles. The only part of me that wasn't covered was my feet, which bore my new missions'-trip flip-flops. We paired up and started on the large window frames. The weather was warm and my stripping buddy was Tony. He was working on the outside while I tackled the inner paintwork. It was hard going. The paint was in thick layers and wasn't budging easily. We slapped the industrial-strength paint stripper on. It was brutal stuff. The smell made me a little light-headed. Were it not for the wide-open window we wouldn't have been able to cope.

'Ouch!' came a screech from the other side of the room. 'I've splattered myself,' said Becky, who had managed to get the paint stripper up her forearm. I went over to have a look. She was OK. A few red specks appeared where the liquid had made contact with her skin. She went to wash her arm under the cold tap.

Over the next couple of hours a few others made the same mistake. Splatters, red-specks, vigorous rinsing. We were trying so hard to tackle the job before our time was up. We had plans to go to a church meeting late that afternoon. I accidentally splashed myself a couple of times, feeling the itch and burn instantly. It wasn't nice, but we wanted to do a good job and leave the windows fully stripped and sanded down.

For a moment, I looked around and thought, 'Have I really just paid all this money to come and strip paint? Is it really worth it?' Tony was chatting away to me from the outside of the window. Tim Hughes' latest album was floating around the building inside.

Then it happened. Tony adjusted the window to get better access to part of the frame. Our tray of paint stripper was pushed clean off the ledge, tipping the contents over my bare, flip-flopped feet.

I screamed then reacted quickly. I didn't even stop to think, but ran like the wind towards the bathroom. 'If I just run my feet under the tap I'm sure they'll be fine,' I thought to myself. I could hear Tony explaining what had happened to the others as I darted into the cubicle and lifted my foot to the tap. As I watched the crystal clear droplets roll away from the arch of my foot, I realized there was no burning, no itching and no redness. My feet were perfect. Unaffected. It was as though the acid had become water in the air before it reached my skin. I tottered back out to the group.

'They're fine! It's just like water! I'm sure that was a miracle!' The group smiled and acknowledged the event. A miracle perhaps?

I returned to my place at the window, my heart racing from the shock and the elation all at once. I picked up my paintbrush.

'Why?' I wondered. Then I felt that voice in my spirit say, 'I brought you here for that – to teach you my power. To increase your faith. To remind you that I can do anything.'

As I reflected, I began to feel a shift in my attitude. This trip was a divine appointment. I'd been brought here into God's purpose and space. This was quality time.

The remainder of our time in Hungary was peppered with similar events. Every church meeting we attended was awesome. LaVere would preach, literally for hours, before praying for people. I went up for prayer several times, and each time felt another layer of my ego peel away.

The group began having similar experiences to mine. We saw the healing of lifelong niggles and health issues. And other things – deposits of peace. We found ourselves laughing all the time. These were times of pure joy together. I felt a connection to life I'd never known.

On one particular morning, I saw things that changed my views forever. We were at a church over the border in Slovakia. It was a very poor area with a large Gypsy population. The people who lived there had very little. And there in the middle of nowhere I watched as a crippled old lady was prayed for. She fell to the floor and her body began to shake (there was no camera, no stage or lights) and after a few moments she leapt to her feet, straightened up with the agility of a twenty-year-old and began to rejoice! (No collection was taken.) It was the most humble of churches and the simplest of meetings. But right here, the power of God had healed an old Slovakian lady's back.

It didn't stop. LaVere began praying for a young man's hearing. He was fifteen or sixteen and hailed from somewhere called the Black City. This city was poor and known for being dangerous. It wasn't a place to take a bus full of white teenagers wearing Nike. Many of that morning's congregation had wandered in curiously to see this fearless older man preaching with conviction about the power of God to heal and deliver.

LaVere drew the young man forward and prayed for him. We thought that was the end of it. But then he drew the boy closer and began to shout in his bad ear, 'Hello! Can you hear me?' It was one of those times when we'd feel ourselves about to erupt into fits of giggles. But to our amazement the boy began to flinch. He could hear LaVere. He was clearly both shocked and overwhelmed.

We passed the Black City on our way home. The place looked like a dive. Blocks upon blocks of stone apartments with no windows, no running water and no electricity. It was the corpse of a communist beast. Filthy children ran around dressed in rags. LaVere had said it was probably a bad idea to go there, being that the crime rate was so high. He advised us to stay in the van. But we looked on as he waltzed boldly through the gates. We watched amazed as the boy from the meeting appeared with his family. He had run back home to tell of his healing. LaVere placed a hand on the back of a young mother and began to pray for the rest of the boy's family. It was remarkable.

I came home from Hungary believing more than ever before in God and his supernatural power to heal. It's a tricky subject. Are people always healed? No, unfortunately not. And there are lots of questions that this section of my story provokes. But as I mentioned before, I believe that these events, these 'signs and wonders' don't happen 'just 'cos'. They have a purpose. They are there to inspire faith and to reveal the power of a living God.

An Audience With . . .

I T WAS approaching the end of October. The nights were drawing in and Starbucks was adjusting its drinks list to suit the cold. I did my usual Wednesday visit to the Resound Office. I'd gradually petered out shifts at the bar until I was able to fill my time with performing. I'd had a cracking leaving do.

After our usual updates on business – gigs that had come in and future plans – Andy dropped an interesting piece of news on me.

'We've been invited to attend the Songwriters Consultation,' he said.

'What's that?' I inquired, trying to sustain my focus. I would often lose concentration in these meetings as Andy monologued his plans for world domination.

'It's a really good conference for songwriters. Artists like Matt Redman and Tim Hughes attend. Just a handful of people really.' I was excited, but a little daunted by the idea.

'It'd be good for you to perform in front of those guys. They do a new song café where people can take the floor so to speak. Just think, you could be performing for Martin Smith and Vicky Beeching!' A little fear rose up in my throat. I'd been singing their songs in church every week and had many of them on compilation CDs bought for me as gifts.

I wasn't sure what to expect, but we went along to the conference a few weeks later.

We walked into the room at the conference centre and took our seats. I craned my neck and looked around. There were about sixty attendees, some of whom I recognized, some of whom I didn't. Graham Kendrick stepped up to the front to welcome everyone, followed by Tre Shepherd, the singer from the band One Hundred Hours. My mind drifted into a hazy memory (picture a fuzzy-bordered dream sequence) of that trip to Soul Survivor two years earlier . . .

A passionate young American with a light husk in his voice was on the platform. Around me were thousands of teenagers lolling in heaps on the cowshed floor deeply engrossed in the speaker's words. He was speaking of the moment when Mary hears Jesus speak at the tomb.

'And at that moment, a *woman* with a *bad past* became the first preacher of the gospel of Jesus Christ,' Tre had said. The words resonated. The Bible was filled with damaged people who'd made history. It had given me hope.

Back in the room, I realized that same speaker was in front of us advising on the location of fire exits. After the introduction, we were each asked to stand and say a few words about who we were. Andy and I were at the back so it seemed to take forever to get to our turn. One by one, these faces gained names and I realized that I was surrounded by the Christian music aristocracy – names from the credits of *WOW Worship 2005*. It got to Andy.

'Hi, I'm Andy Baker. I do some artist development. I also manage Philippa who is beside me.' He gestured towards me awkwardly. 'I also work part-time for my church as a youth leader and worship pastor.' He efficiently listed his duties and sat down.

It was my turn. I stood up sheepishly.

'Hi, I'm Philippa Hanna,' I began. 'I've been a Christian for about three years now. I actually became a Christian at a Godfrey Birtill gig!' I said pointing to Godfrey (who was perched in his casual Godfrey-way a few rows in front).

'Good fruit,' he commented.

'And I just love Jesus. I sing and write songs about it. It's a bit surreal this, because you've all been a huge inspiration to me over the past two years and now you're all here!' A small smile spread across the room.

'And I'm also an animal lover!' I said (a comment directed at someone who had listed cat-hating as a hobby). Instead of amusement as I'd hoped, the comment was met with genuine concern for my feelings – a totally bombed attempt at intro-duction banter. But all in all it hadn't gone too badly. The offending introducer came up to me afterwards to check that I wasn't offended. Oh, well. Christian musicians are all too aware of the pitfalls of offending. (I wasn't remotely offended for the record.)

The last person to introduce himself was Matt Redman. This unassuming character stood, hands in his jeans' pockets, and quietly began, 'Hi, I'm Tim Hughes.' The room erupted. The joke was a little lost on me at that time.

The day was interesting. Some amazing things took place. Over coffee I joined Andy at a table with Stuart Townend. I'm sure I totally freaked him out by telling him he was my favourite songwriter. After cherry-picking my way through several compilation albums I read the credits to find my favourites were mostly by him. He had really fed me as a hungry new believer.

Later, I heard great teaching by Matt Redman on his songwriting processes and things that had inspired his most cathartic songs. Graham Kendrick shared some great insight on his methods too.

That night was the moment I'd been both longing for, and dreading in equal measure. I was a totally and utterly nameless face to this group of musicians. But I was about to sing them a song. Tamsin Kendrick (Graham's middle daughter) was MC-ing the open mic. She was a totally different sort of Christian – edgy and sensual with a real gift for language. She could paint the most vivid picture and evoke all manner of emotions and imagery within a few verses: the archetypal flame-haired, crimson-lipped poet. I loved that Graham had brought forth such a colourful creature.

Tamsin made jokes and read poems between songs. Eventually, she introduced me. I sang 'Higher', one of my first songs about salvation. At that moment I felt some great victory had been won. I'd been so doubtful of myself but had taken the risk. I managed to share my God-given gift of salvation with this great cloud of witnesses and the response was powerful.

Afterwards I sat with a handful of the other delegates. I chatted with Tamsin and Tre about music and worship. We shared visions and dreams and chatted about worship songs that don't know they're worship songs.

'Kate Bush, "The Man with the Child in his Eyes!"' exclaimed Tre. We began to clear out from the bar and Tamsin took a moment to encourage me on the way to our rooms.

Her words were sweet and genuine. She is not a girl who fluffs your feathers for fun; she meant what she said.

The next day was the last. We wound things up with some incredible times of worship. I realized how blessed I was to be there in the midst of that beautiful sound.

As I considered what I wanted the future to hold, I realized that I just wanted to reach people. Graham came over and we prayed about it.

UNCLE G

URING A day of meetings down south, Andy Baker and I arranged to have lunch with Tamsin Kendrick at her flat in London. I really liked Tamsin. She was honest and transparent. She made no attempt to hide what many Christians would die before admitting. Her honesty made us good buddies.

She'd prepared lunch for us. Graham was there too. By now he was like a mentor, a voice of wisdom and experience. This alone was amazing to me. If there was a single person in the entire world that God might appoint as a mentor there couldn't be a better one. He is a sort of folky Christian version of my own father. He's someone who's lived a life in ministry and been a pioneer – someone who has dared to do things differently. After lunch we caught up on our plans.

'And what have you planned for the end of the year?' he asked gently. Andy cut in, 'We have one or two things lined up. Philippa's writing a book,' he began, doing his Andy Baker bit.

'I'm doing a Christmas tour,' Graham started.

'Oh! That sounds amazing,' I chimed in. He slowly and cautiously proceeded to proposition me.

'I wanted to ask if you'd like to come along with me on the tour, as Mary, and Elizabeth. Are you any good at backing vocals?' he asked purposefully. 'It would require taking a backwards step,' he joked. My heart leapt.

'I'd absolutely love to!' I enthused.

December came around fast and it was soon time to pack my bags and hit the road. I met the incredible band one dark night in Tunbridge Wells. The town was a breath of totally different, more expensive, air. We practised for the following two days at Graham's home church. It was beautiful and they made us really welcome.

As I got to know the band I realized I was in superb company. Mark Walker, a keyboard player of high calibre, had played with everyone from Westlife to Beverley Knight. He was tall, handsome and gentle and had a beautiful energy. Then there was Roy, a warm Northern English/Jamaican bass player with soul and warmth. He was a daddy and a granddaddy and an excellent musician. He became 'Uncle Roy' and he was a total rock on the road. He was always up for finding fizzy pop and tasty takeaways at silly-o-clock (a valuable tour ally).

Andrew Small was on drums. He was a breeze of a human being. He'd been MD for bands like Massive Attack and global stars such as Kylie. There was something so humble about him and he knew how to keep good time on and off the kit – a total pro. Finally there was Steve Thompson. He was MD for Graham's band. He had a smile that shone Jesus and a vast overflowing well of musical talent. He'd been an artist but had suffered with vocal nodes. He was now a great facilitator for others and for ministry.

After the rehearsals we began the tour in a local theatre. I was so nervous, wanting to remember every part and be the pro I wanted to be. It went really well. I guess in some ways it was a typical first gig of a tour, but we came away feeling good about it and reviewed things that might need changing after.

Before the second night Graham pulled me aside. 'How do you think the show is going?' he asked. I gave a little feedback and he absorbed my suggestions thoughtfully.

'Would you like to do a song at the opening of the second half tonight? I think you'd be great,' he said. I agreed and from that moment on I played every night.

The tour was an important school for me. I saw how a seasoned minister like Graham does business. He keeps his eye on the Lord. Over the course of the tour we met to pray and worship before every show. In those times of singing Psalms and Scriptures I learned how important it is to 'keep the main thing the main thing' (a Steve Thompson phrase). We got into a rhythm with the ministry, and the shows became more and more potent night after night. Audiences were richly blessed by Graham's clear and genuine sharing of the story of Jesus, from his incredible birth to his death on a cross. The songs were heavy with truth and sense. There was nothing wishy-washy or sensationalist, just pure gentle truth.

I also got to see Graham's work for an organization called Compassion. Every night he gave an appeal for sponsors. I learned that Compassion works in the poorest countries in the world and changes lives by linking children to sponsors. The sponsors give money monthly to meet the child's needs, covering everything from education to medicine. Also, and maybe as importantly, sponsors give love and encouragement that helps lead the child into a healthy well-balanced adulthood. It was remarkable.

Every night they would play a video showing a child's journey and Graham would sing over powerful images of the children he'd met in Africa. I loved the way he used the respect of those audiences to make something eternally good happen. It wasn't simply entertainment or even musical worship; it was serving the Kingdom in a hands-on, real way.

December 2008 was a tiring month. But I emerged a better person. I'll never forget that long, snowy drive home with Uncle Roy, snoozing in the back to the sounds of Chris Rea. We really were 'driving home for Christmas'!

Signed

ANDY BAKER was fast becoming known as the Simon Cowell of the Christian scene in Sheffield (it's a very specific sector to have the monopoly over, but he was managing it). He and Andy Rushworth had been managing The Gentlemen (Joel's band) and doing a sterling job.

The boys had been packing out venues all around Sheffield and their energetic first album 'Smile Back at Me' had made quite an impression. It was early days but they were causing a stir.

The Andys had managed to sign the band to a Christian label in the UK, Authentic Media. When Andy Baker began to talk to them about me, my hopes shot through the roof. I'd just have to make the right impression in a meeting.

As I dressed on the morning of the meeting, I wondered what a Christian record label would like to see me in. I chose a floral fitted shirt I'd found in a charity shop and some denim shorts. That morning as I looked in the mirror I couldn't help thinking, 'You look different today, almost as if your life is about to move forward.'

As we travelled down in the car Andy gave me his usual pep talk. As we pulled up we spent a few moments in prayer. We prayed for God to help us move things forward and to help us reach more people with music.

I was so nervous as the Authentic guy met us at the door. He was a chap named Andy (I'm sorry, they're all over my life). It wasn't like the old days of auditioning, feeling small and inadequate, queuing for hours and singing to empty faces. I didn't feel like that insecure wannabe anymore.

As Andy did his spiel I marvelled at his confidence. He was ahead of his time, giving the big sell to a label on my behalf. He was pitching to experienced industry people with my CD and flyers popping out of every pocket of his satchel.

While Andy talked I sat there across the large boardroom table. I switched off now and again, before coming back to chip in with parts of my story. They liked what they were hearing. I think they could tell we were really determined.

'I think the best thing to do would be for you to hear Philippa sing,' I heard Andy say. My mouth went dry and my heart rate increased. Andy passed me his guitar.

I began to pluck away at the strings. 'Home is not where the broken heart is,' I sang. 'It's not somewhere you feel you are alone . . .'

As we closed the meeting the feedback was positive. Authentic wanted to sign me as an artist and would pay some production costs for the next album. We went for a celebratory drink after the meeting. We were moving forward. That was all I'd ever wanted.

Now all we had to do was create a second album that would help push the boundaries even further.

WRITING TRIP TO WALES

'I JUST might supersede you all with my next album,' joked Andy Baker as he expertly handled driving down country roads. Roo was somewhere behind or ahead of us – I can't remember which. I just remember there being a whole lot of equipment in the car.

We were on our way to a tiny cottage in north Wales – a total hideout. The beautiful old property belonged to the Evanses, a lovely family from church. They were kind enough to let out the idyllic home to family and friends where appropriate.

This trip was owing to Andy's current project – another album of his own stuff. He'd done drums in Steelworks already and the purpose of the trip was to get all the guitars done. The house was quiet and secluded and they'd be able to crack on without distractions.

'Why don't you come along and write some new songs for your album?' Andy had offered. I guess I'd been complaining about having no time to write. There were so many distractions at home and very little space. I wasn't sure whether I'd be able to pull that many songs together. I hadn't been feeling so inspired recently. But it certainly didn't seem like a bad idea so I booked the time out and packed my bags.

I took the bare minimum of recording equipment and lots of warm jumpers. It was still early in the year and many of the roads had ice and snow packed around the edges. The winding roads seemed to take us deeper and deeper into the country through sleepy villages and fields dotted with grubby winter sheep. Finally, we pulled onto the gravel drive of the little house.

From the outside it appeared to be nothing more than a small white cottage. The drive was level with the 'shoe room' as Sara Evans lovingly dubbed the utility space. A small flight of steps led down to the back door. I noticed as we made our way inside that a lovely garden sat opposite the door. The garden was home to a large apple tree complete with tyre swing and bubbling stream.

As we walked inside Andy switched on the heating and the old house quickly began to warm up. As I walked through each of the rooms I could see that great care had been taken in the decoration, paying real attention to country house chic. There were charming pieces of antique furniture in the bedrooms and a sturdy looking stove in the dining area. Traces of family life were everywhere: photographs of kids on autumn walks, snaps from a lifetime of Evans-family holidays. I liked their life.

The shelves were filled with provisions – matches, candles, bulbs, batteries and board games. The cupboards still had some foodstuffs. I could almost hear the family playing Monopoly as I walked into the kitchen. But there were no kids, just Andy Baker and some pre-amps.

'We're probably gonna set up here and in the living room. So, you can write upstairs, or there's the chapel . . .'

'The chapel?' I replied.

'Yes, I'll show you. Just give me a minute.'

Andy took me down the garden and to a small, disused chapel that sat parallel to the house.

'Is this part of the house?' I asked.

'Yeah, this belongs to the property,' Andy said, unlocking the door and putting the keys in my hand. The room was large and had been made-over as a games room. A ping-pong table took centre stage and a few armchairs were dotted around the edge of the room. All manner of sports items hid behind them covered in cobwebs. 'I bet there are big spiders in here,' I thought.

'It's up to you, it's a bit cold.' He wasn't wrong. The mist from our frozen breath was fast filling the room. It was probably colder than outside.

'This heater might work.' Andy dragged an old gas heater over to where we were standing and plugged it in. The building had power at least. And even more interestingly, beautiful chapel reverb.

'Great! I'll have a go at writing in here.' I set up my things and we all ate dinner together. I did a little writing after dinner but the juices weren't really flowing. I was more interested in reading old books and lighting the open fire. Roo and I stayed up quite late that night, chatting over a bottle of wine, talking about music and so forth.

When morning came I awoke to the sound of Roo's electric guitar from the room below. They'd obviously started already. I emerged from the blankets, which piled high over me. There wasn't a duvet in sight, just stacks of blankets. It was 100 per cent old-school country charm.

After a little breakfast I braced myself for the cold and started to leave.

'Guys,' I said, before heading out. 'Could you just pray for me? I'm feeling a little anxious about writing. I just want to have really good songs for this new album.'

'Yeah,' Andy said. The boys came over. They prayed that God would bring songs that would bless and release people.

I ventured out with a hot coffee and plenty of layers. As I sat in silence, huddled by the heater I said one final prayer, 'God I just want to glorify you. And I want to keep going. Keep doing what I'm doing. Reach more people. Help me write those songs.'

I picked up my guitar and decided just to be honest.

A few hours later I emerged with three new songs: 'He'll Still Love Me', 'Work in Progress', and 'Predictable'. They were all honest songs about my struggles to be a good human being. I had no idea what kind of response those songs would get, or even if I'd even dare to share them. But I knew I had to write.

The next day, I woke up singing a melody. By the time I'd showered and brushed my teeth I was singing a verse and chorus. I fleeced up and went down to the chapel. An hour later I'd finished a song called 'Summer Bride', the story of a jilted bride and her journey to realize her true worth and identity in God.

Every time I popped back up to the house the boys were deep in tracking. I played them a few bits and pieces and their response was positive.

By the time the week was out I'd written fourteen new songs and, more importantly, I felt I'd broken some kind of barrier in me.

Dad on Alpha

MY RELATIONSHIP with my dad had improved of late. Certainly there were still tough conversations, but first and foremost my dad has always been my biggest fan and a great support in my life. That's what made the rift caused by my new faith so hard. I hated not having his full respect. I hated him feeling cut off from me. On a birthday card earlier that year he'd written, 'I hope God loves you as much as I do.' It was interesting. It was as if he believed deep down, but didn't want to allow himself to. It was very hard to articulate that God wasn't his replacement. He was the thread that kept us connected forever, if only he could just take that step.

Alpha had been running regularly at our church. The course was always good. The food in particular was *very* good. The course always commenced after an event for interested people. It was an evening called The Alpha Supper. The hearty home-made fare was an easy sell for these evenings. The idea is that members of the church bring along a friend to the evening, and if they like what they hear they can sign up to hear more on the course.

I searched my brain for who might be interested. My friend Amy from All Bar One had said several times that she would be interested in coming along. I invited her and she accepted.

The night before the event, Amy messaged to say she was really sorry but couldn't make it. I shrugged my shoulders. All

I could do was invite her. But then I felt bad. The team would have all that extra food prepared. Who could do me a favour?

'Dad? Hi, it's me. Yeah. I'm fine thanks. Hey, do you fancy a free three-course meal tomorrow evening? It's at church. No, no one's going to brainwash you! I told the guys I was bringing someone but she's pulled out so I have a spare place to fill. It's an introduction to Alpha but you don't have to do anything. Just eat the food. Great! See you at seven. Yeah, it would be great if you could pick me up.'

And that was that. A father-daughter date. Nothing more. I decided to leave my expectations there and get on with it.

That following night the food was certainly on form. Tables were laid beautifully with the church's best crockery, and candles softly lit up the room. We enjoyed every bite of the meal and Dad chatted to my friend Jane a bit. My dad's wit had Jane bellowing her cheeky laugh. It was all going swimmingly, but my teeth clenched a little as Baz rose to speak. Yes, Baz again. He always seemed to show up at a significant moment. He didn't pull any punches when talking about God.

'Please God, don't let this put Dad off,' I prayed silently.

I analyzed Baz's every word. 'I don't think I would have liked hearing that as a non-Christian,' I fretted, gulping my coffee loudly. After Baz finished speaking I breathed a sigh of relief. I looked at the table. There were forms to fill out for those who had enjoyed the evening and wanted to find out more. I cringed at the make-or-breakness of the moment and got up to speak to Jane.

'Yeah I think he enjoyed it – the food at least,' we joked. Then I looked behind me. Baz was speaking with Dad. 'How had that happened?' I wondered.

As Baz moved away, I returned to my seat, 'Have I been targeted here tonight or what?' said Dad, puzzled.

'Not at all. No one even really knew you were coming.' He folded his arms and leaned back.

'I'm gonna have a go at this Alpha thing. I'm gonna have my say. Put my two pence in.' I was astonished. Something Baz had said clearly touched a nerve.

Dad kept to his word. The following Wednesday he went along to the first night of the course. I figured he might as well try, at least. The meal had impacted him enough to check it out. But I didn't expect that he'd go back again the following week (which he did). And again the following week. I eventually stopped inquiring. I decided it was his journey to make and that it would be prudent to stay clean out of it.

The Alpha weekend is pivotal in the course. It comes at a point where guests may want to ask God to come into their lives. Dad had been working his little Irish butt off for the past few years and had barely made time for a holiday. So I was shocked when I heard he'd put aside the weekend and gone away with the group. Joel's dad Phil would be leading proceedings at the weekend.

I let it go and handed the responsibility over to God. If he wanted to reveal himself to Dad then he would be more than capable of moving any mountains that stood in the way.

It got to the Sunday morning of the Alpha weekend. I was at church with Joel, but of course Phil was away with other members of the team. I'd had word from the camp that things had been going 'interestingly'. I wasn't sure what that meant. But Phil was cagey about the details. 'I'll let you speak to your dad,' he said. But after the worship he let it slip, 'Your dad has had an encounter with the Holy Spirit.'

I later heard the story from Dad. Phil had offered prayer for those who wanted to belong to Jesus. My dad had stepped forward and given his life. I pictured the scene: Joel's dad laying hands on my dad's shoulders. What an incredible joining up of dots.

There is more to this story, but some stories aren't mine to tell. I'll just say this – Dad began to change. Some battles arose from nowhere, and for a moment it looked like things had got worse. But in fact, a cleaning process was taking place. It seemed as though God was wrenching things into the open and dealing with old injuries.

The dust settled, and Dad emerged from the fog a sparkling, refreshed version of himself.

DOUBLE BAPTISM

SOMETHING I seldom reference in giving my story is the tale of my cousin Simon. Again, Simon's story is not mine to tell. But it's quite a story. He'd grown up in show business like Dad. Although he was the first-born of Dad's sister Lizzy, he was arguably more my dad's generation.

In the echoes of my childhood memories I see Simon. He was a mild-mannered and attractive young man. He was also musically gifted, and together with three of my other cousins formed The Duskys, a vocal harmony group. They did well, even representing Ireland in the Eurovision Song Contest in 1982.

Somewhere among my memories is the fact that Simon had become a born-again Christian. I mostly overheard tales about his conversion in conversations between my dad and Lizzy. I thought it sounded quite interesting.

But I hardly gave that piece of family trivia another thought, until years later when I found myself a born-again Christian. It then occurred to me to contact Simon. But Dad beat me to it.

Simon had really advanced in his life of faith. In fact, he was now pastor of a large church in Scotland. At the first opportunity Mum and Dad went up to visit him. There were tears of joy when Simon heard the news about our family. After many years of praying for us God had broken though.

I was happy to hear that Mum and Dad had gone to visit. On their return they had lots of good things to say. Dad had found someone who related to his background and his new faith combined. Born into the same unusual show business background they shared a sharp sense of humour and a whole lifetime of experiences. They came back glowing, and they had some good news.

My mum was christened as a child, but just like me, she'd come to realize that public declaration of your *choice* to believe was more important. The sweetest news I ever heard was that Mum and Dad had decided to travel to Scotland again. This time they were going to a baptismal service. And they were both to be baptized. They each made a choice to declare their faith and be baptized by full immersion in water.

They didn't make a big thing of it to us as a family. But when they returned they showed us a DVD of the service. As long as I live I don't think I'll see anything more moving. They each testified about their new faith. Mum spoke of her lifelong interest in God. But she was now choosing to fly the flag and be open about her faith. Dad gave an honest testimony. He said that he wasn't sure where things would go from here. But he now knew that there was hope.

Watching them each go into the water, disappear beneath the surface and be raised up again was more than emotional. I felt like I was watching a movie of my own imagining. It was a miracle.

ENGAGED

JOEL AND I had been ticking along well for almost three years at this point in the story. I can honestly say in that entire stretch we'd never once argued. It's hard to argue with someone who has no interest in confrontation and sees no worth in conflict. If I ever had a problem he would simply listen and try to respond. He had been doing a very good job of loving me.

Joel is a man of few words. He is measured and careful. But one of his little quirks is that he sporadically does things that are totally out of character. The way we got together was a case in point – this retiring character takes me into the forest and tells me we're supposed to be together. Well, put like that it sounds a little creepy, but it wasn't at all. He wasn't someone who would speak or act without careful consideration and good reason. So, I trusted him the day we were on a date in Bakewell and he said the time was right for us to go ring shopping.

We were sitting in a typically English café with a cream tea, and we were chatting about the charity shop we'd just been into.

'I've been thinking,' he said, changing the subject. 'Maybe it's about time we went to look at some rings. I think it's a good time to move forward with our relationship.'

My heart jumped. I'd been dreaming he'd ask me to marry him for the past two years, but this wasn't really a proposal –

more of a conversation about a proposal, so I wasn't sure how to react.

'I was thinking we could go to Meadowhall shopping centre today, if that's alright?'

The next thing I knew, we were pulling into the car park at Meadowhall. With conviction he browsed the shop windows.

'No, that one doesn't feel right,' he'd say, amusing me as I observed a completely generic shop front.

Finally, we wound up in a jewellery shop on the second floor. As soon as we leant over a glass cabinet, a sales assistant appeared. I'd say she was in her mid-forties and she was wearing an impressive layer of face powder.

'What kind of ring are you looking for?' she asked.

'Erm . . .' I stuttered, 'I don't know.' As I said, I had never been the girl planning her wedding since childhood.

'What you wanna do is try and get as much diamond for your money as possible. Don't waste your budget on platinum, you can always upgrade your setting to platinum on your fiftieth anniversary,' she spieled.

My head was spinning. She was talking diamonds and anniversaries and I had left my head somewhere back at the cake shop.

'Have you thought about what wedding ring you'll want?' she continued. 'I don't want you coming back to me in a year's time looking for a wedding ring that doesn't match.'

Wow, wedding ring. This was real. Real, real, real.

As I looked at the price tags, I knew at the back of my mind that Joel didn't have the cash to buy any of them. He'd been plugging away with the band, working hard at trying to get a break, but the problem we'd always faced was a lack of certainty about finance.

'We have a sale on at the minute. If you like white gold I'm sure we'll have something you'll like. I have one that'll look gorgeous on you actually,' said the assistant, ducking into the window display and returning with a tray. It was a sparkling rack of diamonds in white gold and platinum mounts.

'Have you thought about what kind of diamond you want? Square-cut, princess-cut? Do you want one diamond or a cluster? What sort of budget are you looking at?' Joel didn't say anything.

'I don't really know,' I said, feeling a little lost.

'Why don't we have a little sit down and we can show you a few things.'

She definitely saw us coming. I wondered how many couples came in looking as clueless as us!

We were escorted to a small table and the rings were removed from their cosy, red velvet beds. The second ring that went on my finger was a hit.

'I mean this is a really good one because you're getting a great deal on the diamond. Because it is a square cut your wedding ring will fit flush up to it as well,' the lady enthused.

'Yeah, I think that's the one,' Joel said. The lady left us alone for a minute to talk.

'The sale is on for another two weeks,' he said. 'So I'll have to pray about it and find the money from somewhere.'

The romance was dying a little at this point. But it wasn't real to me then anyway. I didn't dare imagine what it would be like to have that ring on my finger for life.

We left the shop and my mind began to wander. We could be engaged two weeks from now. The excitement started to settle in, but there was still the small matter of the money.

The sheriff in me decided I was going to be very annoyed if he didn't pull this one off.

The summer had been a great one playing shows. Two weeks after the shopping trip, I was down in Cornwall with the band for Creation Fest. Creation Fest was one of my favourite events of the year. The Cornish sea-air made everything so beautiful.

That year had been particularly good. The Dawson brothers (Pete and Tim) and I had stayed with a lovely family and had the chance to meet up with friends. I had my very first body-boarding lesson and loved every minute.

One evening, after strolling along the starlit beach, we ended up in a local pub. With a cold glass of Rattler cider in front of me I called Joel. He had a soft smile in his voice as we caught up on the weekend. But it was two weeks since we went ring shopping, and I couldn't help but hint at the fast-approaching deadline.

'It's been two weeks since . . . you know what,' I said.

'I know,' he said. 'I'm nearly there. Just trust me.'

My heart sank. There were only days left for him to buy the ring.

Joel joined us down in Cornwall that year. He was with The Gentlemen at a neighbouring festival, so we met up eventually. A couple of days later we went across to see Joel's sister Lois, her husband Ben and their two children. They live on a farm, which leads a double life as a Rehabilitation Centre for people with life-controlling issues. It's called Gilead and it does amazing things for people at their lowest time. Getting to be part of a community and work with animals really helps people get perspective, learn new skills and get life back on track. We'd visited Ben and Lois lots of times over our three years together and I loved them. They were down-to-earth and easy to get on with.

On this particular trip I found myself confiding in Lois, 'Joel just doesn't seem to be able to get his act together! We've been to see this ring and I'm pretty sure he didn't find the cash in time. It's almost three weeks ago now. The sale's been and gone.'

'Well obviously you're not going to give up on it because you want to marry him! He does need to get a move on though,' she said sympathetically.

I resolved to be patient. I decided I was in this for the long haul, whether or not he had bought the ring.

Two weeks on it was Saturday night. Saturday night had become my night for staying at the Cana residence; it felt like an occasion each week. We'd have snacks with the family and maybe watch a movie. This particular week was not a good one for me. I was feeling hormonal and the small matter of a certain ring had been playing on my mind.

In a private conversation before bed I'd said to Joel, 'You're obviously not serious about this relationship and can't get the cash together for a ring, so I don't see the point in this anymore.'

Joel was silent. He grabbed my drink from my hand and took it into the kitchen before disappearing to bed.

I woke that following morning ready for church and my heart hit the floor as I recalled the conversation. I was flooded by a sudden sense of regret. How could I be so silly? I was supposed to love this guy – and I'd all but given him an ultimatum. I realized that wasn't love. I looked down at a silver ring I'd been wearing for about a year. It had the words, 'Love is Patient' engraved on it. I was wrong and sorry. I just hoped I hadn't done irreparable damage.

Joel said he'd forgiven me. But I wasn't convinced. He seemed a little quieter than usual. I invited him round that night for pizza and he said he'd come. But at 6:30 p.m. he called to cancel.

'Yeah, I'm not feeling too good,' he said. I didn't believe him. He never usually cancelled and he was never ill.

That night I had pizza for one, but struggled to finish even a slice. I was now *convinced* that I'd blown it.

The following Saturday I was practising music at church. Joel emerged from upstairs.

'Hey!' he said, giving me a peck on the cheek. He still seemed a little off.

'I thought we could go somewhere today. Maybe Chatsworth House? It's a nice day.' He definitely wasn't being himself.

'Yeah, that'd be great,' I said.

The whole journey was silent. At Chatsworth we made our way around the shops and food stalls; the atmosphere was still tense. It was as if Joel was looking for somewhere private to deliver some bad news. I wondered if this was the trip that would mark the end of our relationship.

'Do you want some food?' he asked solemnly.

'Err, sure. What about a jacket potato?' I replied, reaching into my purse for cash. He stopped me.

'No. I'm paying for everything today.' I wondered if he was trying to make a point after our conversation. Was this some gesture of financial commitment? A jacket potato? He returned with food and drinks and we ate in near silence.

After a short walk around a kitchen shop we resolved to head back to the car. We walked over a bridge, stopping for a moment to watch the water, the atmosphere as still and as stony as the rocks below. Joel looked over at the river bank.

'Actually it looks nice down there. Shall we have a closer look?' This was just weird. Was he being sentimental? Spiritual? Horticulturally curious? Perhaps he was looking for a place to shoot me! In any event, we began to walk down.

As we reached the water's edge, he kept a few paces ahead of me. I was getting bored of walking.

'Shall we just stop here for a bit?' I asked.

'No, let's go a bit further.' We drifted into our own separate worlds a little. I began picking at the tall grass and looking for fish. Joel appeared to be looking for pebbles. At that moment he stood up excitedly.

'I found a mussel shell!' he said, holding up a broken fresh-water shell.

'OK,' I thought. 'Each to their own.' He carried on looking in the water and within a few moments he had plucked out a second shell, only this one was whole. He passed it to me.

'Check it out. I wonder if there's anything gross in there? I dare you to look.' I didn't much fancy the idea of discovering a live mussel.

'Ugh, no, what if it's all rotten?' I grimaced. 'I think it's best if we just throw it back.' I pulled back my arm, about to throw the shell into the deepest part of the river.

'No!' he said firmly. I froze before lowering the slippery black shell.

'Just have a look. Go on. Trust me.' At that moment my heart quickened. My tummy sickened. Could this be the moment? What if it wasn't? I didn't dare believe it.

I began to prise open the shell. As it opened a couple of millimetres, I was a little scared there would be something alive in there. But then I saw the sparkle.

'What? Is it a ring?'

'Just open it!' I opened the shell up fully and there it was – the white gold band with the square-cut diamond.

'Is this the one? Did you get it?'

'Yep!' he said, pleased with himself. I looked at him.

'Philippa. Will you be my wife?'

'Hell yeah!' I responded, snatching the shiny wet ring and sliding it hastily onto my wedding finger.

I was a stammering mess all the way to the car. Joel stopped to call my parents.

'She said yes!' he exclaimed proudly. On the way home he explained that he'd cancelled the pizza night to go to talk to my dad. He'd taken him out for a pint and everything. It was so strange to picture me crying into my pepperoni while he was asking for my hand.

We walked into Joel's house to find the entire family there. It was an amazing moment. We made our official announcement and showed off the sparkler.

A week or so later we set a date and went in search of venues. We planned to be married in just over a year's time, on 5 September 2009.

Shadow of Death

THE NEWS of our engagement began to sink in and I was beginning to get excited. It was a vivid season. Gigs were going well and we'd started work on the album. But, it turned out there was something to worry about. And it was just around the corner.

The letterhead read 'NHS'. It arrived on the doormat one afternoon a week or so after a routine smear test at my local clinic. The letter said that the test had shown an abnormal reading. I read and re-read the letter. It said I had to go for a further test to check things out.

My first thought was, 'I'm going to die before I get the chance to walk down the aisle. I'm going to die before this album sees the light of day.' It was totally irrational, but equally I knew that life could throw real curveballs sometimes. Two key breakthroughs were happening at that time: the wedding and the album were due to take place within a month of each other, a year from then. A year was long enough to get really ill, I thought. I put the thought to bed and asked for Steph to come along with me to my next appointment.

Steph and I waited in the special pink room. There were lots of pot plants dotted around, but the false sense of homeliness made me feel even more on edge. Eventually my name was called. The nurse sat me in the side room before the procedure and told me what to expect. She told me that these abnormal cells were as a result of something called HPV, and there was no way of telling how that came about. It wasn't necessarily an STI, and it was common in women of my age. It's the kind of thing that if left undetected can eventually turn into cancer. A small procedure to remove and further examine the abnormal cells was required. It wasn't an uncommon procedure, but it would be a little uncomfortable. As she said these things, the gravity of the situation ran a little deeper. I began to feel fear. Part of me wondered if this was going to be the thing to burst my bubble, perhaps it was my past catching up with me. Perhaps I didn't deserve my white wedding after all.

The worst part was having a student nurse look in on the test itself. I usually like an audience but not in this instance! It was an unpleasant process. As the group of ladies showed me the picture of my cervix on the screen they made casual conversation.

'So you won't be having any fun tonight love I'm afraid,' one of them said. I laughed.

'I actually wouldn't regardless,' I replied, and they all laughed this time.

'I know the feeling love,' said one.

'No, actually I have a fiancé!' I said. 'We just don't have sex. We're waiting until we get married.'

'Good for you love,' said the nurse with the speculum.

'I've actually been a Christian for about four years now,' I said.

She interrupted to explain what the image on the screen meant. At that moment I burst into tears. I hadn't cried like that for a while. I'm not even sure where it came from. I think it all just got a bit much.

I dressed and left the room to make my follow-up appointment.

'We'll get your results to you in about two weeks,' the receptionist told me.

'Two weeks?' I thought. How was I ever going to get through the next two weeks?

As we left, Steph and I became a bit emotional. We went to Starbucks and had a bit of a giggle about the situation. I'd just have to carry on as normal.

Meeting the Bear

CARRYING ON as normal while waiting for the test results meant starting work on the album. Tim, Pete, Roo and I felt like a band now. We had a good system of jamming through songs and creating arrangements. I loved those rehearsals in the church. It felt like home. I'd sometimes look up at the stained glass while we were rehearsing and think, 'It's so wonderful that this huge beautiful building feels like my living room. I don't feel like a stranger or even a visitor. It's home.'

On the first day of drum tracking I met Eliot Kennedy. I'd heard lots about this Eliot person. For years his name had floated around in conversations with music friends. He was a huge deal in songwriting and something of a Yorkshire celebrity. I'd certainly noticed that since his return to the Steelworks the place had warmed up somewhat. The walls were covered in gold and platinum disks, bearing all kinds of household names. From Celine Dion to Bryan Adams – and perhaps most excitingly the Spice Girls – Eliot had worked with some of the biggest stars in the industry. He seemed to have a Midas touch.

One cold morning Eliot wandered into Studio One to see what we were up to. I don't know whether he was curious or if he had genuinely come in to grab a cable. But he hovered around for some time. This cathedral of a human being stood tall at six-foot six. He was broad like Johnny Bravo but had no trace of a stoop. His chest puffed out like a proud robin and his voice was like thunder. He wasn't like the producers I'd met before. He wasn't skinny, pale and unkempt with a faint aroma of cigarette smoke (the clichés are true). Instead, he was well-groomed and smelled spicy and expensive. I observed him with interest. Was this what success looked like? Was this what separated musos from moguls? A clean shave and the scent of spiced cedarwood?

Eventually he stopped hovering and moved towards the desk with the authority any bear should have in its own cave.

'Lovely voice,' he said. 'Great tone.' He came up to chat with me for a moment. I can't for the life of me remember what was said. He probably asked me what I was up to. I remember the next line though . . .

'You might be able to come and help me with something actually. Would you be up for that?'

'Yeah, I'd love to,' I responded quickly, not quite believing the situation.

'It'll take you ten minutes – that's all.'

Moments later I followed him into Studio Two. This was the room where I had done my first-ever vocal session and, better still, the room where I had been prayed for by Andy Baker that day. It was also the room where I'd first met Joel. Now it was the setting for my first-ever session with Eliot Kennedy.

Eliot handed me a lyric sheet and began singing me the part over and over.

'That's all it is,' he said. 'Oh, no, no, not again, not again.'

He reset the loop and sang it again, this time with me singing along. 'Alright?'

He obviously had an unshakeable focus. My charm was no match for it. Into the booth I went and was out in less than five minutes (five minutes ahead of schedule).

'Thanks beautiful,' he said, and paid me for the work.

I remember scribbling notes in my diary about that day. Meeting Eliot seemed to be of some significance to me.

I never imagined he'd become a part of my daily life.

Magical Week at the Barn

WITH THE drums and bass recorded, all that remained to do for the album was to track the vocals and guitars. I was to spend the whole week in Preston (staying with my gorgeous friends Tom and Bess) and do the recording with Roo at the barn – Jack and Sue's incredible house.

Being there was like the closing of yet another circle. Once a visitor, an alien, I was now a guest, there on the work of the Lord. We used the attic space, which had been converted into a studio.

It would be utterly boring for me to give you a blow-by-blow account of that week so I'll break it down real quick.

Late nights, rewrites, and pies from a local baker that would blow your mind. Experimentation with guitar parts and vocal harmony. Some daft ideas that stuck (like the crowd noise in the song 'Summer Bride'). 2 a.m. vocals (that needed re-recording afterwards). Lots of laughter and silliness. The result was the fluffy pastry case for my second album, *Taste*.

At night Roo would drop me at Tom and Bess's place where I slept on an inflatable pool bed in the study. It would always start out like a fresh loaf of bread and by morning it had sunk to merely a dustsheet separating me from the floor. I had a stiff neck that week.

Before sleeping each night I read a little bit of Keith Green's autobiography. He had been an iconic worship leader in the seventies. He was a powerful evangelist with a ministry to the lost and broken. He and his wife Melody lived by example, opening their home to anyone who needed love.

I was so inspired by their story. They weren't just talkers, they were doers. They were honest and dangerous and always put the purpose before appearances. It made me think deeply about my purpose.

The sad part of the Green's story is that Keith and their two young children died tragically in a plane crash, leaving a pregnant Melody and their youngest behind. Melody wrote of that fateful morning and the sick feeling she had had about the plane trip. She had kept the youngest behind, feeling that she didn't want all of the kids to go. As she arrived at the crash scene (which was on their private ranch that was also used for ministry), she found there were no survivors.

She wrote about coming to terms with losing Keith and the children. While praying about it she came across this verse, 'I tell you the truth, unless a grain of wheat falls to the ground and dies, it remains only a single seed. But if it dies, it produces many seeds' (John 12:24).

As I deeply considered what the results of my tests might be, I took this truth into my spirit. I wanted to give this album all I had because I was willing to go with whatever God's plan would hold.

TASTE

WITHIN A few weeks, the second album was almost finished. The pressure was intense. We'd done so much to prepare the ground with the first album but the proof of this pudding would be in the eating.

We were on a super-tight budget. It was all we could do to cover basic costs. I focused intently on what to call the album. As I examined the songs they were very different from those on the last record. They were more of a commentary on this new life. With songs such as, 'Work in Progress' I was letting people right into my insecurities. It was a window to my experiences of a new and changed life.

At this point I'll introduce you to Kate, who remains one of the most interesting girls I've ever met. She was one of The Anvil crew. Upon first meeting I wasn't sure if she liked me much. But that's why I know I can trust Kate. She never feigns familiarity or forces herself into people's affections. But once you're in that heart she'll never let you go. She's loyal, sturdy and honest.

She'd known Andy Baker for years and he felt led to involve her in design. She did a few posters and flyers here and there, for which I was grateful. She did most of the stuff for free to gain experience and to serve a positive project. Shortly after the release of *Watching Me* we had a run of T-shirts done with a design of hers. They sold like hot cakes to the girls, and we were left with a box of oversize ones that boys didn't want.

I loved working with detailed, methodical Kate. And I liked having conversations with her too.

One evening, Kate and I were invited to a chocolate-tasting event at a local confectioner's. I'd passed this little shop several times on my way to the church. It was a cute shop set slightly back from the road so it was great for parking. The front was chocolate brown and the sign read 'Cocoa'.

As I entered I was enchanted. The place was a mouth-watering buffet of confectionery boasting endless varieties of chocolate: strawberry, coconut, rum, chilli, white, dark, milk, nut and cinnamon, with every ratio of milk to cocoa. There were hand-finished truffles, fudges and foil-wrapped chocolate hearts. I was melting. But it was a shop of two halves, the back being even more exciting than the front.

Through the small doorway there was an enchanting tea-room. It was more like a treasure chest of trinkets and fancies. As we sat I soaked it in. Whoever owned this place was extraordinary. It was an Aladdin's cave of the cute and the kitsch. The shop sold china tea sets and bunting. The place was furnished with small, elegant pieces of antique reworked furniture and sweet soft furnishings. Every surface had something exciting on it. The back shelves were stacked high with all kinds of tea and decorated by antique sewing machines, cash-tills and gramophones. An eccentric sound drifted up from the needle, some kind of eastern folk record. It was magical.

'Would you like some tea?' one of the owners asked. Two young women owned this sweet heaven. The girls had met at uni and decided that together they would follow a dream to be chocolatiers and own their own shop.

As we tasted chocolate at every stage of its creation and sampled unusual delights, Kate and I locked eyes, 'This would be an amazing place to do a photo shoot,' I said. Kate agreed.

'You could wear a lovely vintage tea-dress.' Kate added, her eyes glistening. As the wonderful evening drew to a close I asked the girls if they'd mind us doing a shoot. Being the creative and romantic souls that they were, they immediately agreed.

The day of the shoot arrived. I booked a wonderful photographer, Chris Saunders. He'd taken pictures of some of my British music heroes and to my surprise he was affordable and local.

We didn't have much time to spare that day. Kate and I went into town to find costumes. First stop was a little boutique on Division Street. It was a box of a shop with hardly enough room to swing a fifties brolly, but I'd often found cute things in there.

We had just begun to forage through clothing rails when I saw it: the cutest dress I'd ever laid eyes on. It was a fitted black number with large white buttons down the front and flared cap-sleeves. I grabbed it hungrily off the rail. Next was a green spotted tea-dress – perfect to wear in a novelty tea-room. I bundled the two dresses into the small make-shift fitting room and prayed that they fit. I couldn't believe it when they both fit me like a glove. I grabbed a hat that matched the black dress and dropped the pile of booty onto the counter. Both dresses and the accessories came in under budget. It was unbelievable. As we left the store less than forty minutes later

I marvelled at the ease of the shopping trip. I can honestly say I've never had one as easy since.

When we reached the shop, I realized we didn't have long. The girls had another chocolate party booked in an hour and a half's time. Kate and Chris helped rearrange the furniture and Chris set up his lighting in expert time. I looked around the room. It was like a movie set. I couldn't quite believe my luck at being able to do this free of charge. I couldn't have made it look better with a million dollars. Chris worked his magic, and in under an hour we had all the pictures we could ever need for the album.

A few hours later I sat looking at what would almost certainly be the album inlay when it hit me: Taste. This new life of mine was sweet, rich, exciting, beautiful and desirable. Like a layer of marshmallow had been spread all over it. All an onlooker needed to do was *taste and see*. And that's what I wanted the album to be – a taste of what life was really like with God at the centre.

That wasn't the end of our involvement with the lovely girls from Cocoa. We wanted to give people a gift for pre-ordering the album and Andy had the brainwave of giving away chocolate. Cocoa gave us an amazing deal on chocolate love-heart lollypops. They were like party favours and we included one with every order. We decided to invite the girls to our album launch to advertise their beautiful wares.

The next time we'd see the Cocoa girls would be at the launch.

COMPASSION

SHORTLY AFTER the tour with Graham Kendrick I began talking with Compassion. By now I was sure I wanted to partner with a charity. It seemed to make so much sense.

After a meeting over pizza with Mal Howard from Compassion it was decided – I would become a Compassion advocate. This would mean I'd use my concerts to tell people about the charity and as an opportunity to recruit sponsors.

A few weeks later, the plot thickened. Compassion made contact. They wanted me to visit a project. The next trip they had planned was to Haiti.

At the time I knew nothing about Haiti, the sister island to the Dominican Republic. It all sounded quite tropical and lovely to me (this was before Haiti hit the headlines in 2010 with the devastating earthquake). Over a steak and ale pie, Matt Harris informed me, 'Haiti is the poorest country in the western hemisphere. As projects go, this will be a powerful one.'

I looked forward to the experience with some apprehension. I'd visited Hungary, but developing world poverty was still alien to me. I had this feeling I'd be affected deeply by the trip.

But first there was the album launch. I would do my first 'ask' for Compassion at the launch of *Taste*. It was intimidating. I didn't want to share the information poorly and put off prospective sponsors. But Matt reassured me, 'It's God's work at the end of the day. Just be yourself and share your heart.'

Eating with the Bear

THE NEXT time I saw Eliot was back at Steelworks. We were doing backing vocals and I literally bumped into him in the hall.

'Hey sweetie!' he said, giving me a kiss on the cheek. 'I'm really glad to see you again.'

'Good to see you too,' I replied. We caught up a little and I returned to my session, but not before he booked me to do some more vocals.

A guy called Jim was at the session. He was another big guy with trendy glasses and an obvious penchant for basketball shirts. I'd met him a couple of times knocking around the studio.

During this session there was a lyric that still needed to be written for the vocal part. Eliot wheeled swiftly over to the computer in the corner and began to type as if pulling words from the sky and throwing them into text-edit.

'The song is called "Temptation",' he said. 'Aw – what's that Bible verse about the broad and the narrow road. Have we a Bible anywhere?'

'I have,' I screeched, thrusting one into his eye-line. But it was too late; he'd already been through the recesses of his vast mental word-bank and pulled out the Scripture. The lyric was finished in moments and I went into the booth to sing it.

As we wrapped up the recording I went in to sit with Eliot. We started talking about the Bible. He wasn't afraid of it, nor of my faith. He told me in fact that he once used the Bible to win a Grammy, (it wasn't put so callously I must add). The song, 'Never Gonna Break My Faith' had been written with a Bible in hand and had caught Aretha Franklin's attention. She'd recorded it for the film *Bobby*, a biopic of JFK's brother, and Eliot had scooped up a Grammy to add to his collection of awards.

As the conversation continued I listened carefully. I shared a little of my story but had a feeling that there would be another conversation. As I was leaving that day I mentioned my new album. Eliot asked how it was going and I told him it was finished.

'I'd love to play you some of it,' I offered.

'Yeah, absolutely.'

We settled on going for dinner the following Friday followed by a trip to the studio to listen to some stuff.

When I next saw Joel I ran it by him. Of course, I had to make sure he was cool with me having dinner with Eliot. He was a fella after all and dinner can mean many things. In Joel's usual relaxed manner he approved.

'You can look after yourself,' were his exact words.

So, I joined Eliot that Friday at the Ivory, an upmarket bar-diner in town.

The Magic Vicar

ON THE day of dinner with Eliot I had a photo shoot. Again, it was with Chris Saunders, but this time we were bound for the Peak District.

Chris and I planned to get some new promo shots. The sun was shining for the first time that week. Although the weather was fine, the ground was soft and sludgy. Chris was using his incredible eye to scope out locations and spotted a picturesque suntrap beneath nearby trees.

'Come on,' he said. He was a man of few words but they were usually well chosen. He'd known since our first shoot that I was a Christian. He said he wasn't religious.

'Oh no, my new shoes!' I shrieked as I ambled behind Chris, carrying his camera bag under my arm. My white flats were filling up with mud as we waded into the glade. The wind picked up and it was all I could do to keep wisps of hair out of my mouth. We settled in a clearing, my feet now freezing with the cold sludge.

'There goes my clever summer purchase,' I thought, mourning the pretty white wicker shoes.

Chris began clicking away, but with only two of us at the shoot it was proving tricky to get the lighting right. Chris pulled out a gold reflector and made an attempt at one-armed clicking. It wasn't easy.

'We need a miracle!' I joked!

Just moments later a rather distinguished-looking gentleman in a formidable autumn hunting jacket walked past.

'Hello there,' he sang. 'What are you up to then?' It was a bit embarrassing really – a guy and a girl alone in the forest with a camera.

'We're just taking some promo shots,' I quickly assured him. 'I'm a singer-songwriter.'

'Really? Oh, that's charming. Would you like some help?' He waltzed over and took hold of the reflector, listening to Chris's directions. While Chris clicked away I chatted to the helpful chap. He revealed that he was none other than the local vicar!

Later, with the shoot wrapped up we joked about the 'divine intervention'. Right at the moment we needed help, none other than the local vicar had shown up in the middle of the woods.

THE BEAR HEARS 'TASTE'

THE BEAR and I sat down to a yummy dinner at the Ivory and became fast friends. It turned out that we had the same birthday and had even made our debut performances on the same stage in Skegness. Our dads were both club acts and we'd grown up in awe of the stage and of music.

There was a moment during dinner when Eliot mentioned that there was something 'different' about me. I told him outright, 'I think it's Jesus.' He thoughtfully stroked his trademark facial hair with interest.

'Interesting,' he said.

After dinner, we made our way to Steelworks, nattering all the way. Once in the cave, the bear fired up his system and loaded my CD onto the computer. I thought he might cherry-pick his way through the album. But instead he cranked the volume up to 11 and listened to every song – *every* song without interruption. My heart was in my mouth. After the playback he looked me in the eye.

'I'll do whatever I can to make sure people hear this,' Eliot said.

I couldn't believe my ears. To have the approval of this giant meant so much to me.

We had breakfast a couple of days later at a small café overlooking the lake in Millhouses Park. It was beautiful. As we chatted some more I handed him a gift. It was a book I'd just read called *The Shack* by William Paul Young. It was a special book. He received it with grace and said, 'If you ever want me to introduce you at a gig or anything just let me know.'

It was a timely offer. We'd been planning a launch for the album at The Mega Centre in Sheffield. It was a step of faith because the venue was big. Even with support and promotion it wouldn't be easy to fill. But things seemed to be coming together.

'It would be amazing if you could introduce me at my album launch,' I said to Eliot. I gave him the details and prayed he'd come.

The night of the launch I was nervous, but more than anything I was excited to share my music. I believed in the album and in the vision. It was hard to believe that just a few years ago I'd been at the end of my rope, hopeless and without joy. As I waited to start the show I looked out at the auditorium. It was full. Eliot took to the stage and gave a gushing introduction. What he said blew my mind. I had to pinch myself.

The show was magical. It was amazing to look out onto the crowd and see the guys from the studio and my family. When the time came to do the Compassion ask, all my fear disappeared and from somewhere I found focus. Sponsors for twenty-six children signed up at the event. It would prove to be the start of an incredible relationship with the organization.

WEDDING BELLS & HONEYMOON

T HE NEXT big event on the calendar was perhaps the biggest of my life: my wedding day. Any married readers will relate to the tension that comes with planning a wedding. Between rehearsals for the album launch I'd been ducking out for ceremony rehearsals and to *Taste* wedding cake. See what I did there? It was certainly a jam-packed couple of months.

A few days before the wedding most of the work was done. We picked up the rings and twisted and turned them on our fingers. These rings would be our symbols of marriage to the world.

As if planning a wedding and honeymoon wasn't enough, Joel also had moving house to take care of too. After collecting the rings, the next thing to do was to bundle my bedroom into the back of his car.

Joel had already moved into our new place, breaking in new cutlery and awaiting my arrival. He'd found homes for our engagement gifts in anticipation of our life together. It was a strange feeling. The wedding was so near, yet it still seemed so far away. With less than a week until the big day it seemed almost unbearable to leave the new place. But we were serious about our decision not to sleep together until we'd tied the knot. This was a view I'd found so challenging and unconventional before coming to faith. But with God it seemed more like a beautifully wrapped gift that should be left under the tree, despite the buzz of Christmas Eve.

I spent a final night in my own bedroom and was picked up the following day by my dad. It was good to be back in my parent's nest, the house I grew up in, with home-cooked food and nostalgia. It was a strange, dizzy feeling.

The night before the wedding was definitely a highlight. All the ladies came round for pampering. We drank champagne and giggled like Carry-On characters. My friend Jane came over to do our nails. I sat in my parents' living room and felt truly wholesome. I even got out my posh ivory underwear for my eighty-year-old aunt to admire.

I had a decent sleep and awoke at 8:30 a.m. I didn't feel nervous at that stage, but I was giddy with excitement that the next time I saw Joel he'd be standing at the altar. As well as never having slept together, we'd never been on holiday as a couple. We had never seen each other naked. But there had always been chemistry.

I had been impressed with Joel's purity, despite our close-ness and future plans. He had self-control. It helped me to believe that he was truly passionate about me, and not just about my body. But of course we were looking forward to the wedding night. I was slightly jittery. There were lots of firsts around the corner. I had also received the all-clear after my scare at the clinic. The treatment had worked and there were no more abnormal cells. It was such a relief. Nothing could eclipse the excitement of our impending marriage.

The morning of the wedding brought classic Hanna family chaos. With eight of us using the bathroom it was a lengthy process. Everything from showering to putting on garters was somehow a shared experience. An hour before we were set to leave the real chaos began. Drivers, photographers and video guys arrived, seemingly in hoards. I sat at the table trying to do my make-up while the others ate bacon. I was too busy to entertain the idea of breakfast. The kids flocked around fizzing with delight at the grand white gown, hanging like an angel's wings in the front room.

When I finally put on the dress the heavy fabric felt like a house around me; I could barely rotate in my mum's living room. The ladies yanked at the lace-up bodice until I was safely inside the spaceship and ready for lift-off. Mum handed me my bouquet and the front door was opened revealing the car and the video man.

After some fumbling with the dress we managed to get me into the back of the Mercedes. Dad held my hand as we drove. As we pulled up to the church I glanced at my reflection – this was how I would look on my wedding day, the pictures we'd show our kids. I was glad I'd bought the good mascara after all.

With some help from the mums, we finally began the procession. As my dad began to walk me down the aisle I could have sworn he was trying to drag me backwards. Perhaps I was walking too fast.

'We have to reach the altar before that minor chord-change,' I thought. 'You can't reach the altar on a minor chord. It'll create a sense of doom.'

I saw Joel's smile. He looked amused and giddy. I felt the glow of my friends and family as they supported us. The service was beautiful. My friends played my favourite worship songs and the Dawson's dad, Nick, did the service. It was personal and real.

The reception was gorgeous too. The food was amazing and the speeches made us laugh and cry just like they should. I was too nervous to eat. It seemed fitting that I give a speech. The wedding represented a lot of things in my mind: my union with Joel, yes, but also a huge celebration of how a life lived in faith becomes full of joy and goodness. I looked around the room to see 120 guests, most of them new additions to my life since becoming a Christian.

One corner of the room lit up for me. It was the table with my old boss Andy and his fiancée Anna on it. I was so grateful to have had a good manager during that season. He was a significant part of the puzzle of my life. He made it possible for me to go out and sing to people. Beside him were Andy and Sharon Rushworth. They had been so important to me as a new Christian. Andy had been the first to make me sing in church. He'd opened that door and inspired me beyond belief.

Next to those guys were Chris and Shan. I could hardly believe that just a few years ago I had been singing at their wedding. I remember looking at Shan as a beautiful bride and wondering, 'Will anyone ever think I'm marriage material? Will I ever be good enough?' Now here I was on the top table, my parents Christians and my parents-in-law pastors. I felt as if this banquet was a hero's welcome into the Kingdom of God. I deserved nothing, but I'd been given the best.

At just after 11 p.m. my new husband gave me a nudge.

'Can we go yet?' he said. I agreed. It's really not like me to leave a party before it's over, but this was different.

Now, some details about a wedding should be left private of course. But it's important that I share something with you – it was worth the wait. I felt like a healing took place as we shared our very first night together as a married couple. I began to see sex as something different – a spiritual and physical union. It was the beginning of a new family.

As we arrived at the airport the following morning I glanced at my ring several times. I felt strange. A bride, a wife, a grown-up. Joel guided us towards the gate. I looked at him. Did I feel safe? Could he really look after me? I suddenly felt scared, as though we were all alone and expected to know what we were doing with ourselves! All the hustle and bustle of the wedding lead-up had subsided. We were husband and wife.

Once we arrived at the resort in Tenerife and began to settle in I felt determined to enjoy myself. This was our honeymoon. We should be swinging off chandeliers, making friends with locals and skinny-dipping in the sea. In fact we were fairly quiet and tired and spent ages trying to track down sun-loungers. The honeymoon was a lot of things. It was our first chance to work as a team, looking after our time and money. Joel kept the euros in his wallet and I spent them for him, cocktail by cocktail. We filled most of our days lying by the pool working on a tan to show off at home.

I'm not sure whether this neurosis is mine alone, but I suffer from holiday anxiety. Something happens to me when I try to relax in unfamiliar surroundings. First, I begin to wonder whether I'm having enough fun. I always hear other people's holiday stories and marvel at their carefree abandon. Then I begin to feel lazy and unproductive. I start to imagine that all this relaxing is going to have a permanent effect on my work ethic and I begin to wonder if I'll ever be able to afford another holiday. All of this, coupled with my new 'wife' status, and trying to visualize our new life together left me feeling a bit out of sorts. But towards the end of the holiday the pressure began to lift. As I imagined rejoining my friends and family and living a normal life things seemed less crazy. Joel and I had begun to laugh more and had made some amazing new friends.

Barry and Margaret were a godsend, quite literally. We were almost sure that this sixty-something couple from Kent were angels. They came to share our table on a packed evening in the outdoor bar and chimed into our conversation. That was it. Once they knew that we were on our honeymoon they began to share with us – stories about their family, jobs and their married life. They were on an all-inclusive deal at the resort meaning that they were entitled to as many drinks as they liked. So, they insisted on sneaking drinks for us. From that point on, they brought us something every time they saw us. We tried to pay for things, but they insisted. Then Barry decided he wanted to take photos for us. Up to this point we only had arms-length self-taken photos of the two of us, but Barry insisted on capturing us in the pool together, drinking cocktails and sharing some fun with them too. They sent us the photos on CD the week we arrived home.

PART 5
ADVENTURE

In at the Deep End

BACK TO real life – it was time to get back to work.

I'll be honest, I've never done much writing with others. But when Eliot Kennedy asks you to write a song, you don't say no on the grounds of insecurity, you give it a go. So, I had a writing session booked with the bear. He gave me a great start to a song and I took it from there. I couldn't help but flutter when I heard echoes of wonderful songs in the voice memo.

It so happened that a friend of mine, Abby, had just got married. Her new husband was Chris Eaton – another award winning writer. Andy had been catching up with them and suggested we do some writing together. It happened the same week that autumn.

The Eaton household felt like a home – a home that very good songwriting had built. The morning I began writing with Chris I wasn't feeling too good. We went down to the studio after breakfast and I pitched up with a notepad and my guitar. I played him a couple of songs that he seemed to like. When we found an idea to work with we got started.

He bashed through chords and ideas on his keyboard. It was clear that this man was a real talent. His success was no accident. He was inventive, clever and gifted. But I began to freeze. It felt like ideas were getting stuck in my throat or in some filter between my ears. I made contributions, but they were sparse. We eventually finished the song we'd started hours earlier, and there was a bit of a cloud in the room (or so I imagined).

After lunch the three of us went back to the studio with the intention of writing something fresh. I hid in the downstairs loo and said a quick prayer.

'Dear Lord, help me get my stuff together here. I'm freezing! Just help the ideas to flow. I want to glorify you. Help me uncork this thing!' I wandered back into the room with a little idea on my lips.

'Before we do the worship thing, I've got this one idea. I just have the verse at the moment, "I don't wanna waste any more time in the mirror" and so on. Perhaps when we get to the chorus we could say something like "I am *amazing*". But not that of course.' Chris looked at me.

'Why not that?' he said. I pondered.

'Would I dare say that? I am amazing? I guess that is the whole point – learning to believe that fact,' I said, my thoughts now making sense.

The session took on a life of its own from that moment. It was magical. The words and melodies threaded together easily and we were left with something that felt special to me. I had an inkling that this was a song many people would relate to.

Days later I went home and recorded the first acoustic demo of 'I Am Amazing', closely followed by 'Ave to Love'. As I played them to Andy Baker at the office we reflected: to have found ourselves in the company of such talent, something good must be going on.

Trip to Haiti

JOEL AND I began to get into the swing of things with marriage. It was challenging and scary at times, but we loved working as a team and I was starting to enjoy wifely things, such as cooking (not that I had much flare).

Apparently no one has ever seen God. But the closest you can get is in the faces of those who work with the poor and destitute. In November 2009 I visited Haiti with Compassion. I'd only been married for a couple of months. It was a big trip for me, my first to a developing country with huge cultural differences and extreme poverty.

Compassion did their best to prepare us for the trip. But nothing could really have prepared us for what we saw and experienced. I thought I'd include my journal of the trip. It tells the story by itself. So, here it is . . .

Day 1

The journey to Miami

The journey was long and tiring today. I completely slept through my 4:50 a.m. alarm and wound up with twenty minutes to shower, dress and get out of the door. Joel drove me to the train station and waved me off from the platform. Then it was sleep time, with bright and sharp commuters bustling around me. The journey was steady and upon arrival at Heathrow I met up with Dez and Ken (from YFriday) and we bought some last minute bug-sprays and bottled water for the trip. Tour leader Mal joined us just as we boarded our flight to Florida. The ten-hour flight was comfortable. I was sleepy, but enjoyed three films including *Up*. I've found that I'm missing home already.

In Miami I feel compelled to soak up every moment of the comfort and luxuriance of western culture: large portions of sugary food, water you can brush your teeth with and toilets that flush.

Day 2

And so to Haiti

We began our journey at 6 a.m. local time and we're now flying across the breath-taking aqua-coloured ocean towards Haiti. From here it looks perfect and stunning. It will be interesting to see what it looks like up close.

Wow. Today has been intense. As you drive from the airport the first thing you notice is the number of people. They're everywhere – hundreds and hundreds of them, and they're all selling things – from mangoes swarmed with flies to second-hand socks. No one actually seems to be buying anything though. There are heaps of rubbish everywhere and animals tearing their way through it all.

The hotel is situated out of the centre of Port-au-Prince. The locals aren't allowed past a certain check-point, which makes it safer for visitors, weird. Armed guards met us at the hotel, which by any standard is stunning. It's surreal to see something so amazing after driving through the grimy chaotic city. I'm not complaining though.

After lunch today our first port of call was a local orphanage. Down dark, dusty streets hidden behind a huge iron gate was the tiny enclosure. Once through the gate a bunch of children awaited us. The two groups, visitors and children faced one another. The children sang us a welcome song. I felt the tears forming already as I scanned the face of each child, thinking, 'these kids don't have a mum. They don't belong to anyone.' We weren't prepared for what happened at the end of the song. As we clapped in gratitude they raced towards us, each one making sure to kiss us and grab our arms. They were so hungry for affection. An eleven-year-old girl whispered half-English, half-French questions into my ear as we walked around their humble home. I mainly nodded, not quite understanding. We went to her room so she could find us a picture she'd drawn. She lived in a small, hot, square, empty room, with only a bed and a small box with a comb and some other small trinkets. The door was nothing more than a bed-sheet. We left soon after and the children seemed confused by our fleeting visit. This was our first encounter with Haitian children. Afterwards we visited the Compassion office and heard from the staff about their various roles. All I could think about was getting back to the hotel.

Day 3

Seeing Compassion in action

So, today we began by visiting a Compassion project. We were able to see first-hand what Compassion actually does. They do something different in every project. Whatever the need for those children, it's catered for. However, the project's main components are generally:

- School-like facilities which the children will visit about four times a week. Compassion provides 75 per cent of school fees for project children
- Extra vocational training at the project studying various trades and additional skills. They learn how to sew, cook and make things to sell
- Church and teaching about Jesus

- Free healthcare including all the necessary vaccinations and medication
- General mentorship and love
- Compassion Haiti's vision is to produce healthy Christian adults who can build a better Haiti.

It all makes sense now!

We joined the children in their church service and it became a welcome ceremony for us! After hearing them all sing and testify about Compassion I offered to speak to them via a translator. I ended up singing 'Amazing Grace' and the children sung along in Creole. Good old 'Amazing Grace'. Irish singer Brian Houston wound up the service with one of his songs. After we'd been shown around the rest of the project we were split into two groups to visit the homes of sponsor children. This was our chance to see where these children actually come from.

In Haiti everything half-decent seems to be built upwards and out of the centre. The closer you get to the centre, the darker and dirtier things seem to become. We were led by a bodyguard down narrowing streets. We passed an old woman dressed head-to-toe in black. She was selling charcoal in a dark doorway. We had all kinds of strange looks – a bunch of white people coming to observe the poverty. The walkways turned into sort of sheltered alleyways with small rooms branching out from them. The streets seemed to get hotter and darker and the stench of human waste and garbage became overpowering. Finally at the very end as we were enclosed into a corner was a small doorway with a couple standing in it. This was the house! Their clothes were well worn and the heat was dripping off them. The woman held a baby. We could see that the door was a hanging sheet and the house was nothing more than a small room. At the back of the room hung another curtain, behind which was another room with another house, another family. We asked a few questions via the interpreter. Then a girl jumped out of the curtain dressed in her pristine blue Compassion project clothes. She was one of the most smiley and cheeky children from the church that morning. It's hard to believe that this joyful, lively, well-turned-out child lives here. Her parents look fed-up. I'm already beginning to realize that Compassion is the only source of light for this family. They tell us they're grateful to God for what Compassion does for them and ask us to pray before we gladly leave.

Even though I'm seeing all of this, I still feel quite self-focused. I think because I am here on my own I feel quite needy. Lord, please help me to get my mind off myself and help me to absorb what you're giving me here in Haiti. Please break my heart for these people. Amen.

Day 4

The nightmare trip to La Gonave

Today was very tough. We journeyed to an island called La Gonave. I'd heard that it was very basic and we'd get to witness the more rural side of poverty in Haiti. We planned to stay in a Wesleyan Mission (no creature comforts there). But first we had to get there, which meant travelling by land and sea.

The journey was mostly idyllic. As we drove to the port through the countryside I felt myself breathe a sigh of relief. The packed, garbage-covered streets of Port-au-Prince make me feel quite claustrophobic and the humid air carries its heavy smell right into your lungs. The air con of the van and copious amounts of bottled water were our only escape.

We arrived at the port expecting to find a ferry with an on-board gift shop. In reality, our vessel was nothing more than an old wooden boat with a weathered sail and half a foot of water in the bottom. It did have a motor though, so the crossing would only take a couple of hours. A couple of us needed the toilet after the bumpy van journey. We forced ourselves to brave a hot shed with something resembling a latrine inside. Emerging from the dark, fly-infested room we smothered ourselves in sanitizing gel (another new best friend) and set sail.

The water was calm, the sun was beating down and I had a cold can of cola in my hand. What could be better? As I stared into the horizon the most magical thing happened. Dolphins! Five or six of them leapt in sequence in and out of the water. I stood on the warm wooden hull of the boat clinging to the ropes and singing along with Brian. We noticed that Dez was looking a bit green, so we said a prayer for his travel sickness. Soon though, it became clear that he was more than a little unwell. As we docked we could see he was distressed and complained of pins and needles in his hands and feet. We drove the half-mile to the mission. As we arrived Brian raised the alarm, 'Dez needs a doctor right now, he's having chest pains and can't breathe.' Dez staggered inside and was taken into a back room.

A group of us began praying, but fear was building. I felt the Lord prompt me not to let the fear take hold, but to pray and keep declaring that God had the victory. As people came out of the room from seeing Dez, their expressions said the worst. 'He's really suffering' someone said, 'Where the heck is this doctor?' said another. A Compassion doctor arrived and said that we should wheel him straight over to the hospital. Fortunately, the only hospital on the island was seconds away. The nurse prayed for him immediately and they began giving him all manner of jabs and drugs. Eventually he came round. Meanwhile we were still praying at the mission. When we heard he was stable, the people at the mission served a traditional Creole meal. I took care not to eat the salad or take any ice in my drink as usual.

After tea we went without Dez to the project on the island. The children were so full of life. They laughed and sang and danced. In this dusty, barren island, bright, lively children gathered and received everything they needed. We ended the day by eating dinner with some sponsor children. We've been moved to a basic hotel with air conditioning, as Dez is still feeling unwell. The hotel is very, very basic. Very. Basic.

Day 5

The toughest day ever

Today was one of the toughest days I've ever survived. I didn't sleep a wink last night due to a chronically bad gut.

At 6 a.m. as the team arose to get ready, I was still awake – exhausted, ill and feverish. Something I ate yesterday was obviously very wrong. I spent some time crying, praying and texting my mum. Eventually I managed to get myself together, take some Imodium and set off to the project. There were two vehicles: one air-conditioned, one not. I took some dehydration fluids and sat in the air-conditioned car. Visiting the project was hard work. It was the hottest day so far and the heat in the church was unbearable. We stood, drenched and tired, as the local people sang songs of honour to their guests. The amp was buzzing at a deafening level. We were asked to sit and a woman from the Child Survival Programme stood to give her testimony. The Child Survival Programme is another thing that Compassion does alongside child sponsorship. They look after pregnant mums, giving them antenatal care and teaching them how to look after their babies.

A woman called up her four-year-old son and testified through the interpreter, 'Before Compassion I had lost several babies. Compassion took me in and looked after me. They gave me care; they helped me with my pregnancy. They helped me to feed my baby and gave him medicine. I must say thank you, thank you, thank you.' She was shouting by now, 'I worship God first but then you, you are second to God for saving my baby.'

By now I had cracked. My self-pity started to drain away and I felt completely humbled. She continued, 'If I could lift you all up on my shoulders and carry you around this village I would! Thank you, thank you for everything you do.' I was so moved.

Afterwards, feeling hot and weak, we walked through the blistering heat into the heart of town. Children surrounded us, following from the project. Each wanted their turn at holding our hands. A teenage mother handed me her baby dressed in a fancy purple frock and began speaking to me in Creole. I think she wanted my wedding ring. Either that or she was asking to marry me! The children all giggled as I made faces and blew kisses at the bemused baby.

We arrived at the house we had come to visit. The people who had followed us waited at the gate and we went in. The family brought out their only chairs, falling apart and unstable, and sat us in the shade at the back of the house. The mother stood at the slanted tin door and awaited our questions. Two of her children were being sponsored and stood beside her in their pristine blue uniforms. She tells us that eight people in total live in the house. The entire house is no bigger than my front room. It's only big enough for two large beds. The children all share one bed. The cooking area is just a sheltered area outside. It's immaculately tidy but really they have nothing: a small pile of sheets, some pans and a couple of products beside a bare hairbrush.

After giving some small gifts we leave. We continue down the road, parting to allow a donkey through on his travels. This time we found ourselves at a slightly more sturdy, though not much larger house. This one was home to nine people: a mother, father, grand-mother and six children. They offered us information about the family. A relative sat on the floor close by with her baby. As we chatted to the family I noticed she was holding up her baby for us to see. The baby had a huge tumour at the base of her spine. After praying for the family we offered to pray for the baby. Before we knew it, other families began gathering to ask for prayer. We ended the day by taking a boat back to the mainland and driving to a nearby hotel. Thank God for Imodium! The location of the hotel is beautiful. Praise God for protecting us and giving us some kind of respite from the trauma. I can't help feeling guilty that I'm this grateful for a comfy bed and air con after what I've seen today.

Day 6

Seeing children survive

Today seemed like a long day, but with less packed in than yesterday. We made the three-hour trip to Gonaives. We visited a church (yet again hot as heck). This was a much quieter morning, as we were mainly meeting mothers and babies. They crammed into the hall, dressed in their smartest clothes to welcome us and testify about the Child Survival Programme. I had no idea that Compassion was doing all of this. Not only do they work though child sponsorship, but also they help so many children by protecting them before birth. I'm beginning to see the vision now. This organization sets out to be the hands of God, wrapped around the infant, even from the womb, and holding the child's hand all the way through childhood and into adult life. It's a fantastic vision for a nation that is clearly without vision.

We played with the children for a while. They light up at the smallest of things: balloon animals, face paints and bubbles. They're so cute. After eating a brief lunch at the pastor's house things began to stir again in my stomach. I really began to feel the heat and was overcome by feeling sick. I had to go and lay down in the van just to feel the air con and sit still. I wasn't able to move much without feeling nauseous so I missed the final appointment of the day. The team visited a Complimentary Intervention Programme (CIV). A CIV is where Compassion will intervene with a particular area of need in addition to everything else they do. In this case the intervention was a water-filtration system for the community.

After the visit we made the three-hour journey home. I only started to feel better about an hour into the journey and it seemed to be a God thing. I looked beside me and saw a gift given to us by one of the mothers in the Child Survival Programme. It was a painted wooden plaque reading, 'God, protect my family.' I felt myself well with tears, deeply humbled.

This mother lives here, surrounded by the challenges of unemployment, disease, poverty and hopelessness. Yet she desires that God would protect my family.

Day 7

Filming the appeal and meeting the hope of Haiti

Today was our last day in Haiti. I had to film my appeal for child sponsorship. It was so hard. On the bank of a colossal rubbish tip and surrounded by unfriendly looking locals I had to list the things that make Haiti hopeless, while they all looked on in disgust. Staring straight down the lens I tried to imagine rich people in church pews with more than enough cash to change a child's future. I suddenly feel desperate to shake people out of their sleep. It's too easy to ignore reality; I've been doing it all my life, even with the best of intentions.

Looking for filming locations we drove through what's said to be the worst slum in Haiti. We thought we'd seen the worst but nothing prepared us for this. It was like hell. People were living and trading surrounded by piles of rotting garbage, their wares crawling with insects. People sitting on rubbish dumps and children were picking their way through it for food. There were more people than I've ever seen in one place, literally climbing over each other. The buildings looked like they'd just been hit by a tornado. They were falling apart, hanging by threads, some even charred and black, with people living in and around them. Everywhere we turned there was filth and chaos. It was dumb-striking. Children tried to grab our attention begging for anything we might give them. We were told not to open the windows in case the bus was swarmed. So many people could easily turn it over. For the first time I feel like we're surrounded by an entire community that's barely alive. It's dark and disturbing.

After our drive we came back to the hotel to have dinner with the Leadership Development students. These are exceptional students from Compassion projects who have been awarded support to go to university. We shared a meal with a number of students who have achieved degrees in sciences, languages and computing. All of them claimed they'd be nowhere, perhaps even homeless or working as prostitutes, if Compassion hadn't intervened.

After the students had left to go back to their homes, the team gathered in the foyer for a final drink together. I couldn't help but notice a number of prostitutes venturing to and from the bar. I'm now convinced that poverty isn't the root of the problem here. There is a spiritual poverty that the country can't escape. Jesus really is the hope for these people and Compassion offers his love.

Day 8

The journey home and reflections on the week

Well, I feel completely wrecked. This week has really taken it out of me on every level. I've been disturbed, afraid, sick and humbled. I've felt alone at times, and been confused about what makes me secure. The depth of what I've experienced is hard to tell right now. When I imagine what I've seen: beautiful children without mothers, families with so little, people living, scavenging and working in rubbish surrounded by pigs and stray dogs, even prostitutes in our beautiful hotel, it's safe to say that my heart is well and truly broken.

It seems so wrong. We see people clamour around our minibus some of them hostile, some excited and some just begging. Then we are whisked away to the safety of our hotel and fed nice food.

Despite the heaviness of this nation, so many live in hope for a better future. You see people dressed in their smartest attire, Bibles under their arms, strolling through the filthy streets to have their faith renewed at church. I only pray that I'll take this new perspective with me and make it worth something. I know that Compassion are working with over a million children worldwide and about 400 children a day become Christians through being shown God's love in this way. Now I have to add to that number!

Band on Tour

I TOOK a week off after my return from Haiti. It was necessary. I was still sick. Whatever bacteria had found its way into my body wasn't going anywhere fast. Also, I was a little shell-shocked. I needed time to process what I'd seen and experienced.

Joel and I continued to settle into married life. One of my big concerns was keeping afloat financially. It's amazing to be a musician, but it's also a scary lifestyle at times. We really never know how we're going to make ends meet.

But God surprised me with what came next. Kate and Andy Baker had been busy in the office. They'd been planning a tour for me with the band. I thought it was quite a big ask really. They wanted venues to fork out to pay us, as well as covering tour expenses, such as a full PA and sound engineers.

I was genuinely shocked when Andy called excitedly to tell me the tour was booking out thick and fast. When we got together at St. John's to go through the new set I was giddy with excitement. More than twenty venues had invited us to play.

In our usual positions in the corner of the church we bashed through new songs. It was threading together amazingly. And this time we had the added bonus of a sound team. Dave and Tom from Big Blue Box became our new best friends. They rigged up all their kit in the church for us to rehearse with.

It was an epic rig – a whole big blue lorry full of stuff. There were large flight cases with my name on. This had come about by a miracle in itself.

A chap named Ronnie Fernihough had come to our rescue. His passion was to provide artists with the technical requirements they needed to put on a great show in Jesus' name. He gave us the rig at cost price to fit our budget.

After rehearsals we went into the back room to pray. We prayed and asked God to bless the tour. Although we had no idea of his plans, we wanted to fulfil them.

The Ground Shakes

THIS NEXT section is a challenging one and I share it at the risk of putting you right off God. But believing in God and that he is good relies solely on seeing a bigger picture. We can't see that picture if we censor the sad parts. So here it is.

It was a drizzly Wednesday morning and I was making the bed. I guess it was about 11 a.m. I was about to go to the Resound Office for a catch-up. I was thinking about the 'Ave to Love' song I'd written with Eliot. I hadn't really done anything with it yet. Eliot had loved the demo. It definitely had something special about it.

My phone buzzed. As I picked it up several messages appeared. The first was from my mother-in-law, Yvonne: 'I'm so sorry about Haiti. Praying.' I suddenly felt a little cold. Was she just speaking generally? I'd spoken to her a few times about what I'd seen there. But it seemed a little random six weeks after the trip.

I opened another message. It was my mum, with words to the same effect as the first message. Now I knew something was wrong. I went downstairs and flicked on BBC News 24. My heart flipped as I read the headlines.

A MASSIVE 7.0 MAGNITUDE EARTHQUAKE HAS STRUCK THE CARIBBEAN NATION OF HAITI

The extent of the devastation is still unclear but there are fears thousands of people may have died.

Haiti's worst quake in two centuries hit south of the capital Port-au-Prince on Tuesday, wrecking the presidential palace, UN HQ and other buildings. The earthquake occurred at 16:53 local time on Tuesday, 12 January 2010.

It was surreal. I flicked between stations – every channel was reporting this disaster of apocalyptic proportions. I recognized streets we'd walked down just weeks earlier. My mind quickly moved onto the projects we'd visited, the beautiful children we'd met and the great work we'd seen. Was it all lost?

Andy Baker called me. Haiti is a forgotten territory. The local press wanted to speak to someone who had been there recently. It was strange. Months earlier, I knew nothing about Haiti. Then I went there and it became the only thing I could think about. The whole world was watching the scenes of devastation.

I gave interviews all afternoon and finally landed back at the office. The news reported that the death toll was rising every few minutes. Thousands were searching for their missing family members. I thought about Moses and Jeannot, our hosts on the trip. Were they OK? The thought of them dealing with the chaos, rubble and bloodshed was horrible. Seeing everything they'd built fall to the ground would be gutting. Where was God in all of that?

I knew that something had been deposited in me the moment I became a Christian. Some call it optimism or positive energy. I know it to be hope. It says in Corinthians 13 that there are three things that last forever: faith, hope and love. I thought about the earthquake in this context. It didn't make sense to me that God would allow such a terrible thing to happen to an already barren place. But the hope inside me won over the doubt. The earthquake didn't make sense to me, but God had a plan for glory in this devastation. Now there was an opportunity for the church to do something awesome.

I thought about whether there was anything I could do to raise money for the emergency fund. Then a plan began to form in my mind. 'Ave to Love' was a song about never giving up, always praising and believing in the resilience of life.

I called Eliot and told him I wanted to record and release the song as a charity single.

'Babe, I get it. Let's do it,' was his exact reply.

The next day we were at the Steelworks tracking the single.

By that time we were almost ready to go on the road with the band. As we prayed before our first gig I had a revelation. These gigs had been planned in advance for us. God had known that there would be an earthquake in Haiti. He'd known that help would be needed and that it would have to come through ordinary people. Here was our chance to do our little bit.

We put together a video about Haiti to play at the gigs. It was deeply moving. The images of the earthquake brought sadness. But the images of aid reaching the homeless, of survivors being found alive weeks after the event and of Christians singing and praising God on the shattered streets brought hope. Watching the video I had a revelation: love is the only response to a question we can't answer. We'll never know *why* some things happen. But we know what we can do. We can love people.

The song didn't sell a million copies. But on each date of the tour we played our video and it encouraged nearly 100 people to sponsor children. Only heaven knows what the ripple effect of that kindness from strangers in the audience will be.

For me, it was a fantastic learning experience. The events of life don't always make immediate sense, but there's so much we don't see. Through experiences like the above I've had the tiniest glimpse of God's heart. He wants us to intervene.

BACK TO SCHOOL

OUR FIRST Christmas as a married couple came
and went. But as the tinsel came down so did the
snow. Early January saw inch upon inch of the stuff
billowing onto the roads and weighing down the trees. Crisp
flakes settled into layers of frosting over Yorkshire.

As I looked ahead to the coming year, I was relieved to see
that work had been coming through. Now more than ever
Joel and I had to rely on our faith to get us through. Both of
us were self-employed, but despite our anxiety about money
God was sustaining us.

As I looked at my diary, one item glared at me: 'Schools'
Week'. I'd never done anything like it before. I was going to go
into schools (real schools – just like the one I was suspended
from) to teach music and talk openly about my faith. It seemed
like something a qualified individual should do, not the girl
who scraped through her GCSEs and whose tutors were mostly
glad to see the back of. But it became even more intense when
I discovered one of the schools was my *actual* school. For me,
school had been a terrifying academic and social minefield. I
made all kinds of compromises to feel safe and included there.
Now, everything was different and I was going to have to face a
whole assembly full of kids just like the old me.

Schools' Week arrived and I went to stay at Mum and
Dad's to be closer. I awoke on Monday morning and looked

out of the window to see a snowy duvet covering the road. A phone call came at 8:30 a.m. to say that the school I was meant to be going to that day was closed. I laughed to myself. For five years I'd prayed for school to close. Now on my one week back in town the snow was keeping me away. I was slightly relieved and resolved to eat toast and marmalade in my pyjamas, just like the old Philippa, while GMTV bubbled cosily in the background.

But Tuesday arrived and so did Becky. She came to the door in her Ugg boots. Becky was about my age and was also a Christian. She worked for something called the Cross Project.

We hit it off straight away and she put me right at ease. We spent that day at a school in Wakefield where I taught music to various ability groups. It all went off without a hitch. In fact, I quite liked it.

'Maybe I could do this teaching thing,' I thought.

But day two was the real challenge. I was taking over an assembly to talk about my faith at Horbury School – my old school.

If I cast my mind back to school assemblies, my recollection painted a scary picture: a large old hall with ancient trophy cabinets; a sea of teenagers tucking in shirts and being told to *shush*. I was once a timid new girl, shuffling around in shiny shoes, trying to make friends and be invisible all at the same time. I couldn't believe I was about to do the Philippa Hanna music thing in this context.

Walking into my old school I could see it was a different place, quite literally. The old building had been bulldozed and replaced by a state of the art facility.

In the hall, I set up my guitar and a lectern with notes for sharing my story. I was feeling nervous; my mouth was completely dry. At 9 a.m. the kids began to file in. Pretty soon all the chairs were filled. My former music teacher Mrs West (who I learned was also a Christian) introduced me.

'Now then Year 8,' she said. 'I want you to be respectful as we have a very special guest here with us this morning. Philippa is a former student who is now a successful musician. She has a very interesting story to share. I want you to be on your best behaviour.'

I looked at the group. They were tiny, not scary teenagers, just kids really. I had a sudden revelation. My school years were hell at times. I had times of fun (towards the end), but many times of isolation and fear. This was my chance to tell kids who felt that way that there was hope.

I sang my songs and talked about how God had impacted my life. But mostly I talked about how there was hope and that I truly believed that whatever they were going through each of them was special and there was a plan for their lives. The phrase: school – the best years of your life hadn't applied to me. It was only now, a decade after leaving that I was finally fulfilled and had a strong sense of self-worth.

The response was wonderful. Kids came to talk to me afterwards and I realized that any encouragement given to this age group was invaluable. I should have known that – I'd craved it so much myself.

As Schools' Week ended, I reflected: God seemed to be a master of closing circles. A lost young person, once removed from this school, had been invited back as a guest to share a story of success and joy.

To me, that seemed like a miracle.

THE ABANDONED CHAPEL

I GREW UP in kind of a rural area. I say 'kind of' because in fact my old road is right off the M1 motorway. Just a couple of crop fields separate the redbrick semi and the busy motorway. Also, the quaint long row of redbrick houses looks out to a very busy main road. But at the other side were endless hills. What was a black pit stack in the eighties had become lush swells of green in the nineties. There were farms, fields and woods – endless territory for curious kids to charter.

But that was over the road, and as a kid I learned that the road was of great danger to my life. It was loomed over me like a precariously suspended dagger. '*Don't* go near that road! The cars come down it too fast,' I was told. I was so afraid that the first attempt I made to cross it saw me frozen in the path of an oncoming vehicle. I was grounded after that and banned from the fronts of the houses. It was just as well really. Playing chicken was too tempting once the thrill of road-crossing had been experienced.

I didn't venture much beyond the tarmac runway for many years.

Haigh, where we lived, was home to a dozen children who shared a playschool, and on becoming teenagers roamed hopelessly without much to do. When we grew a little older we exhausted the usual hangouts – the park with its impressively high swings and slide, and the plantation, which functioned as nature's assault course and smoking den.

We'd sometimes venture down the road less travelled – the mouthful of gravel pathway that led to the chapel. The chapel was disused. It was in decent nick save for some cosmetic stuff. A lady who lived on our side of the road was apparently the owner. It was quite spooky. Peeking into the dusty rooms through the large windows we would tease each other with the large cobwebs around the heavy frames. But despite the ghost stories it seemed there was nothing sinister there, only its former life as a meeting place for Christians.

Some weeks after Mum and Dad had given their lives to God I was back at the family home. Mum casually mentioned that they'd had a visit from a minister called Raymond. He was in his autumn years with a full head of wavy white hair and a sparkle in his eyes. Dad was new to church talk, but apparently Raymond had laid it on in full force. He was banging on about the Holy Spirit, healing and the nations. Dad wasn't sure about it all, but Mum was quite impressed.

The main topic of conversation had been the chapel. Raymond claimed he had heard a word from God to: 'Go to that church in Haigh and open it up.' So he had. And now he was sitting yards from it in my folks' house, drinking tea.

The chapel had lain to waste for decades, and just weeks after the house across the road had become home to two born-again Christians, new life was breathed in. Over the weeks that followed Mum and Dad became pillars of that little church. It became a charity shop and was once again a place of worship.

Back at Sheffield Christian Life Centre things were busying up. We'd moved services into a local academy. One weekend when all the worship leaders were out of town I had the chance to lead. It went incredibly well and I began to fall in love with leading people in song. It felt so different to performing. It was so experiential. I'd find myself zoning out of reality and into some other space where I'd suddenly get perspective. I'd leave feeling liberated and rested.

Our weekends grew busier. Gigs *and* worship leading meant most weekends were full on and I lost track of what was going on with my folks. One weekend I resolved to take Joel over to Haigh to see what was going on at the little chapel.

I took my place in the pew. The innards of the chapel had been spruced up a little. Thanks to Mum and Raymond's wife Daphne the place was looking warm. Raymond stood up without any warning and kicked off proceedings. There was little structure but there was something incredibly refreshing about the service. My heart welled when Dad got up to lead the songs. Perched on his foldaway stool with its blue leather seat, he played his Godin guitar and sang gospel.

The songs were quite retro. But when Dad sang them they just sounded classic. It felt like I was listening to a Johnny Cash album. To my left was Mum banging away on a djembe drum. I took stock for a moment at the scene. Only months ago Mum and I had prayed for Dad with a deep longing to see his heart refreshed. Now here we were – all together in a building that itself had been in a deep sleep.

It seemed that wherever God was invited, dead things would spring back to life.

WHAT WOULD KATIE DO?

I LIKE KATIE PRICE. Before you slam the book down, I *challenge* you to hear me on this. Yes, she is a glamour model. Yes, her language is far from ladylike. Yes, she comes across as hard and she has built a brand on what is essentially stripping her clothes off. But, what I like about Katie is this: she'll always have a go. She knows she's not a singer, but if someone offers to make her a recording star, she'll give it a shot. She'll perform live for the whole of Europe. She's the 'author' of several bestselling romance novels. When questioned about the books she said, 'Of course I don't write them. I don't have time to write books.' Is she a fraud? Or just an opportunist? To me she's an inspiration. She makes me realize that if you're fearless there's pretty much nothing you can't do.

She was the first person I thought of when a message popped up on my phone one evening: 'Babe, if I can get you the vocal coach job on this Hong Kong project would you be up for it?'

It was Eliot and the Hong Kong project was *Project Lotus*. I'd heard Eliot talk about it before. He was plotting away with a former Disney boss to put together the 'Asian Spice Girls', the first-ever pan-Asian girl group.

It was a pretty big project. Eliot and I had done a bit of writing for the girls. But since then he'd put together a writing camp where people like Gary Barlow were going to turn out hit songs for the finished band. He was about to go on a trip to Japan, China, India, Korea and the Philippines to find five outstanding girls per territory. They would then be brought to an academy in Hong Kong where the whole process would be filmed for a documentary series. That's where they'd need a vocal coach.

I stared at the screen. Hong Kong was a long way from home. Joel and I hadn't been married long. It would mean six weeks away from home.

I'd had lots of conversations with Eliot about my career. He always believed in me and had one eye on opportunities that might move me in the right direction. He wanted me involved in *Project Lotus*.

In the next room Joel was getting into bed. He's not a late person, though he tries to stay awake while I watch re-runs on TV. I slipped into the bed beside him.

'Eliot's offered me the vocal coach job on this Hong Kong project,' I blurted out.

'Do it,' said Joel.

'It would mean being away for maybe six weeks.'

'It would be great for you. Do it.'

The phone was in my hand.

'Yeah, I'd be well up for it!' I texted back.

Eliot contacted me soon after. He'd landed me the role. It was a little daunting. I'd done some private tuition but this was a different thing altogether. I would be coaching rooms full of talented young girls with a dream. I would be in Hong

Kong living and breathing a TV show. It would be my job to keep the girls on form vocally – a real responsibility.

But I'd be working with a world-class team at the centre of a groundbreaking project. When I asked myself, 'What would Katie Price do?' I knew the answer.

A couple of weeks later, Eliot began to talk about the academy. We had a conference call with the project head, Jon Neirmann, and the academy manager Laura. We discussed timetables, elimination shows and flights.

It was a big plan. Eliot had visited all five territories by now and had met the girls. He told me how talented they all were and it made my heart race with anticipation. These girls could really be the next big thing. He had me record vocal exercises for them that would be downloaded onto their iPods for rehearsal every week. And so I moved on to the next chapter.

Project Lotus

IT'S LATE SEPTEMBER and I'm in Topshop with my mum looking at summer clothes in the sale.

'It's going to be roasting in Hong Kong,' I say, piling summer T-shirts and dresses over my arm. I still can't quite believe it's happening. Six weeks away from home. Joel got me a webcam and Eliot helped me get Skype up and running so Joel and I can speak every day. Before I know it, Eliot and I are stepping onto a plane for the long flight.

I'd never flown business class before; I never really imagined I would. As we step beyond the red curtain and into our seats I can hardly contain myself. The chair goes horizontal for sleep and there is every TV show and film imaginable on the console in front of me.

Eliot is beside me. It's an early flight and the sun is still coming up. As we settle in, a hostess places champagne into our hands followed by a menu. Beside me on the seat is a wash bag. 'Toothbrush and eye mask,' I think. I actually *squeal* as Molton Brown cosmetics sit in orderly fashion within. Eliot laughs at me grabbing his chest as he usually does, as though each time he laughs is the first and the sensation takes him by complete surprise.

In that strange place between time zones Eliot talks to me about his dream for the academy and about just what a big deal it could be. He tells me how he became a writer and the various peaks and troughs of his journey. It's inspiring. I look out the window and feel as though I'm in a dream.

We arrive in Hong Kong around teatime the next day. We're met by cameras as we touch down. Journalists want to interview Eliot about his recent trip around Asia. I'm in the toilets trying to de-flight my fringe. Thank God for dry shampoo in a spray can.

As we make our way to the head office of FarWest Entertainments I realize why they'd put us in Business Class – so we could sleep and be ready for work on arrival. Too bad I spent the whole flight watching movies and going through my posh toiletries.

Jon Niermann's office is exciting. It's full of mementos of his time working for Disney, alongside framed pictures of him with politicians and sports' stars. There's a playfulness about Jon, as you'd expect from anyone who's worked alongside the world's most famous mouse.

We eventually make it to our apartments and begin unpacking. My stomach flips with excitement as I find my way around the compact flat. It's flawless and well designed. If you imagine a home atop a skyscraper in the most densely populated part of the world, I'm sure you'd get quite close to what it is like.

The apartment is clean and tasteful. The cupboards light up when you open the doors – they are like refrigerators for clothing. The apartment manager shows me round, pulling out handy kitchen equipment from every corner.

'Your yoga mat is here and you can take out DVDs at reception,' he says.

'OK,' I think. 'I'm glad I know where my yoga mat is. I don't know where I'd be without my yoga mat.' The table and chairs fold into the wall. The kitchen has a single two-ring hob and a hidden microwave beneath.

As I fall asleep between the crisp white sheets that night, my dreams are interrupted by anxious thoughts about the academy. I can't put my finger on what exactly I'm anxious about. Perhaps it's thoughts of my own auditions in the past: the adrenaline, excitement, self-doubt and rejection.

The next evening I meet Brian Grant. He is filming the show. I first judge him to be a forthright forty-something cameraman. I quickly learn that he is about to turn sixty and is a Grammy award-winning veteran director and videographer. He's worked with everyone from Olivia Newton John to the Muppets. His enthusiasm is contagious. This is a man who lives to be excellent. He has a wonderful quirky habit of writing down things that amuse or inspire him. And he is the voice of the camera, always speaking up for the finished product, anxious for its wellbeing like a proud stage Dad.

I know this is going to be something else . . .

THE ACADEMY

THE FIRST MORNING of the academy got off to a questionable start. I'd barely slept for nerves and excitement, going over every way I knew to bring the best out in a singer. I began my morning by poking myself in the eye with a mascara brush. Coupled with long-haul dry eye I couldn't open my eye for the next hour or so. The idea of having a camera pointed at me didn't exactly appeal at that point.

Eliot came from his apartment to collect me. He said a quick prayer over my eye and we hit the street, walking towards the MTR (Hong Kong's infallible answer to the tube system). We made our way to the gleaming government building where the academy was being run. The building was used for many educational purposes. It was suitably huge, a dozen interesting things going on.

After a morning meeting with the team I was led to my room. A radiant Australian who was the Art Director had decked it out beautifully.

A piano had been ordered for me to use. Minutes later the room was filled with Japanese girls and film crew. They didn't all speak English.

By the end of the day five groups of girls had come through my classroom. Each group was from a different Asian country and they were all so different. I was learning quickly about the cultural differences. The Indian girls were bubbly and friendly and giggly and loud. Every one of them had a smile. The Japanese and Korean girls were very focused and professional. The Chinese girls were lively and loud. The Filipino girls were warm and talented, but quieter.

At the close of the day I began to realize what a massive task I was about to undertake. Friday came around quickly and it was time to see the girls perform for the chance to stay on for week two. It was manic. Although the team was wonderful and Eliot worked his magic with the groups, we were all running on adrenaline and faith. There was an audience and a TV show to consider. We watched with bated breath. To our joy and relief the girls (and the team) pulled it off.

Seeing those girls come together from all corners of Asia was magical. At the end of the night we had to send the less suitable girls home. They had sad faces and broken hearts. This was going to be tough. I knew what it felt like to be in their shoes. Some of them had come from poor provinces and had nothing promising to return to. But we were only there to find *five* girls. We couldn't keep them all.

The weekend gave us all some time to reflect. Hong Kong was electric. It's a place where moping seems impossible. A metropolis of opportunity and wealth, it sort of beckons to you as you walk through the street.

Before long, Hong Kong started to feel like home. I loved the hustle and bustle of the city streets. The higher up you go, the quainter and more Chinese the city becomes. Our apartment was up a hill, beyond a winding stairway of boutiques and small street markets. As we reached what was essentially the high street, we passed all manner of fish shops and delis. The smells hit me in the face as I walked through the crowds each day.

Sundays were our day off, so Eliot and I took a walk down by the docks. It was like discovering the Emerald City (in shopping terms). I was born in Barnsley and live in Sheffield so I'd never crossed over the threshold of a Fendi or Prada store. My trips to London have rarely taken me to Knights-bridge and even when I'd passed through the sight of a doorman freaked me out. What if he wouldn't let me in on account of my ordinary handbag?

I soon figured out that Eliot was quite at home in a posh shop. He'd strut ahead like a bouncer, dwarfing the awestruck Chinese people in his path. Eliot looks tall at the best of times, but surrounded by the residents of Hong Kong you'd be forgiven for mistaking it for Lilliput. I was quite at home there and enjoyed not having to reach too high for things in the supermarket.

As we walked, Eliot talked to me more about his life, his career and his music. It never ceases to amaze me what this man has achieved. He has a positive energy, a faith that makes things happen. Walking around this great city my heart resounded with the intoxicating beat of possibility.

Monday came and we convened in the office to discuss the week ahead. Brian was there with his camera as we reviewed the files of each remaining girl. We bantered and argued and discussed each and every positive and negative attribute. It became like an obsession.

'Did you see how well Rachel coped under pressure?'

'Did everyone notice how much the kids liked Nikita?'

Sometime after those conversations had drawn to a close John casually said, 'Why don't you play at the next gig Philippa?'

'I'd absolutely love to!' I said.

'I think you should. Show these girls what they're aspiring to be,' he said.

My mind began to buzz – what should I sing?

The week got into full swing and we planned the elimination gig. I gradually grew to love each girl so it was horrible to consider any of them leaving. But we soldiered on. The girls were getting better at singing and dancing, mastering harmonies and being put through their paces by the incredible dance teacher and Olympic skating contender, David Liu.

When Friday came around the girls did a great job. There were some surprise performances and others that confirmed our suspicions.

It came to my turn on the mic. I was so nervous. I'd been hammering vocal disciplines to the girls and now I had to demonstrate the skills. Talk about pressure. But when it came to the moment I knew what I wanted to say.

'It can be so hard not to compare yourself to others, especially in this situation. So, I dedicate this to all the girls here. No matter what happens tonight, you're amazing,' I said. Then I sang, 'I Am Amazing'.

If the only reason I went to Hong Kong was to tell thirty young women they're amazing, I did my job.

FANCY MEETING YOU HERE

THE FOLLOWING WEEKEND a complication with our visas came to light and Eliot and I had to return to England. I couldn't believe it. No sooner had we got into the flow than we were flying back. But I had to admit it was a relief. I'd get to see Joel and bring all the clothes I had forgotten the first time around. I'd also get to experience business class flights again. More free fancy toiletries. All good. But before we could go home we had to make a small detour . . . to the Philippines.

Problems with immigration meant that the Filipino applicants hadn't all made it to Hong Kong. After they'd made two failed attempts to travel, there seemed to be only one solution – to go to them. Joel had flown out to see me in Hong Kong, and shortly after he touched down it was decided we would both fly out and audition the girls there.

So, we were in the Philippines days later. And boy, were the girls talented! My eyes were opened to the incredible untapped talent that is in the Philippines. All the girls were special singers. We came back with three clear contenders. And, after the detour back to England, we were ready to hit the third week.

Of course, the delays meant that we would be in Hong Kong for much longer. The trip would stretch right to the end of November. I'd get home just in time to buy some Christmas presents. But I couldn't wait to get back to Hong Kong.

On our return we had to move apartments. This time we were in a more commercial part of town. It was like living in central London, but cleaner and more user-friendly. By now the weather had calmed, but we could still comfortably walk outside without a jacket. From my apartment window I could see Starbucks and McDonalds. I went to one or both of them most days. I grew to love walking to and from the MTR station and became well aquainted with the shopping malls and boutiques. I fell in love with the warm air and the mellow city vibe.

When I worked at All Bar One I spoke to my colleagues about faith on a regular basis. The beautiful Alex Gorvorusa was one of these colleagues. We often sat and drank tea and I would tell her about how God had changed my life. She was gentle and neutral and open-minded. She had a boyfriend too, who was equally mellow and easy to talk to. One of the things I'd always mention to people was this 'coincidence' thing. I found that the frequency and potency of coincidence in my life increased amazingly when I asked for God's guidance. Still, what happened one morning as I made my way to the academy blew my mind.

I was about to go through the station turnstile to the platform when I remembered I needed to top up my travel card. I queued for a moment then bundled some dollars over the counter to the lady. As I thanked her and turned back to the barrier, a familiar face caught my attention. My jaw fell to the floor.

'Alex!' I screeched. She looked my way immediately and returned the shocked expression.

'Oh, my God, I can't believe it!' she cried. 'What are you doing here?' Shane was close behind, his face draining of colour. He clearly thought it was a freakish coincidence. We moved from the path of the people traffic and chatted.

'I'm here doing a girl band project, a TV show thing,' I explained. 'What about you?'

'Well actually, we're only here for the day. We're teaching English in mainland China and we've come on a visa run.'

I shook my head. Alex wasn't even living here. It seemed like a one in a million chance.

'I can't believe it, this is so weird,' she said.

We got over the shock and chatted for a few minutes. I mentioned that I thought it was a miracle and we resolved to meet up once we were all back in England.

When I arrived at the academy, the team was blown away by the coincidence. It's hard not to believe in a higher power when things like this happen. If life is a game of odds and science and probability, then where do these things leave you? Alex and Shane were in Hong Kong for one day. They could have travelled to the MTR at any time that day, but they were there at the exact moment when I was about to get on the train. If we were travelling in the same direction I may not have seen their faces. But because we were crossing paths I couldn't miss them. If they had chosen a different turnstile I may have missed them in the crowd. But we were right beside one another at exactly the right moment.

It's moments like this that make me think there's a designer somewhere, a great planner. I don't believe that we're puppets on cosmic strings. But like a great personal assistant, if we give over our diaries to God the schedule will dovetail perfectly.

He can organize meetings we don't even know we need and bring about the right people at just the right moment.

I believe that God puts certain people in our lives for a reason and we're inextricably connected. Whether you're in the same city or on different continents, you'll stay connected until you've fulfilled your purpose in each other's lives.

Errors in Judgment

BEING AWAY from Joel was hard. We'd talk on Skype after my day at the academy was over. But often I'd be exhausted as it neared midnight and Joel would be eating his tea. I began to feel a little isolated. It didn't help matters when I fell ill. My wisdom teeth were coming through and the gum around them became infected. To make matters worse, the antibiotics made me feel awful. Instead of socializing after work I started to go home as early as possible to rest. It meant that I felt quite separate from the rest of the team.

At this point I began to feel a little odd in a music industry sense. I wasn't sure if I was strong enough to handle it. Conversations about what made a girl suitable for the band left me feeling a little strange. The bright lights of Hong Kong had dazzled me a little – it was such a commerce-driven place that was focused on finery and money. Surrounded by the immense beauty and talent of *Project Lotus* my confidence took an unexpected nose-dive.

During the second leg of the competition I began to feel more and more uneasy. The atmosphere was very tense. The project was gaining attention from influences outside. We had ten amazing girls left and among them there was some really fine talent. Plans to get them ready for the finale and the attention of a large audience piled on the pressure. But I was happy. I thought I couldn't fail. I was there to judge and to coach. How wrong I was . . .

Throughout the project, Eliot and I had largely agreed on which girls were doing best and those who sadly didn't cut it. But the finale gave rise to some huge differences in opinion and the team was divided. In the decision room, the judging became heated. We also had some new guest judges who had different opinions, and this confused the rest of us. Some girls had pulled it out of the bag on the competition night, throwing our prior views out of kilter.

As we thrashed out the pros and cons of each combination for the band, I became aware that Eliot wasn't happy with what I was saying. It must have been a shock, as we'd pretty much agreed up to this point. A palpable mist of quiet fury hung about him.

After the event, we gathered at the after party. Drink in hand Eliot stared into space. He was upset with some of the things that had been said in the deliberations. He was emotionally invested in the competition – we all were. Because I hadn't agreed with him in the judging room I felt like I'd disappointed him. The days that followed were grey – a mixture of anti-climax and confusion. Eliot and I talked via email. We were both upset. It was a hugely isolating experience for me. I can't explain the feeling. I felt as though I'd failed, as if I'd made some huge error in spiritual judgment by going on the trip in the first place. When something doesn't work out as hoped, it is easy to ask whether it was the right thing in the first place and whether God was really in it. I tied myself into a knot thinking about it.

The dust settled and right before my departure back to England Eliot and I met up, hugged and reconciled. True friendship can survive anything I guess. But I left Hong Kong feeling deflated beyond belief. It just wasn't the all-singing all-dancing return home I expected. I'd hoped I would be taking away some important connections and stories of glory and victory. It wasn't quite the report I was carrying.

The saving grace was the time I'd spent with the girls and the connections we'd made. At that moment that's all I had to treasure from the experience.

Picking Up the Pieces

JOEL CAME to fetch me from the airport. I was tired, and felt grubby after the long flight. I'd had a six-hour wait in Dubai and had snoozed through the calls to prayer in the airport.

Finally I was waiting for Joel in Starbucks on home turf. England was covered in a thick duvet of white snow, the most we'd had in decades. Joel's warm, indiscriminate embrace met me and I fell into it. I was shell-shocked, disappointed and on a huge comedown from the adrenaline-fuelled trip. I was still smarting with the sensation of having been some kind of disappointment. Although Eliot and I had patched things up, I still felt really weird about what had happened.

As Joel and I walked out of the airport the freezing-cold air filled my lungs and knocked me backwards as we made for the car. Within twenty-four hours I had the flu. I spent the next week indoors. It gave me time to process.

It was then that I thought about my list of miracles. I went into the study, sat at my computer and began to write this book. I was at another low ebb, wondering what God was doing and if I'd failed his plan. I didn't have much work booked in. The trip had taken me out of performing for the best part of two months. I didn't really feel like me at this point. But I looked at my list. And I saw a God who was at work in my life. I had to believe now more than ever.

As I began working through each incredible thing that happened in the last few years, it lifted my spirits and built my faith. I may have made mistakes, but there was something called grace over my life. And God wasn't ready to throw the towel in. So, I decided, neither was I.

OUT OF THE BLUE

CHRISTMAS CAME and went. We sang the New Year in and it was time to start a new project. I called Roo.

'I really wanna record an acoustic EP,' I said. 'I'd really love it if you'd be involved.'

'Great,' Roo said. 'Do you want all the bluegrass guys involved as well?'

I hadn't thought about it.

'Err, yeah?' I said, thinking on my feet.

We did two days of rehearsal. There were five of us in total. Banjo, mandolin, bass and of course myself and Roo. Eliot produced the project and once again I felt the warmth in our musical friendship.

It was the first time I'd recorded songs like 'Raggedy Doll' and 'Happy in My Skin'. By the time I had the CD in my hands I was in love with the results.

The EP was ready just in time for another tour. We were going out as a band again. As we travelled around the country we were encouraged that people were turning up to see us. There was a momentum. People loved the new songs.

As we travelled around I had lots of time to process. I realized that God had been in the time in Hong Kong. He is God even when things don't turn out as we expect.

On that tour I began to feel like myself again and I remembered the privilege of sharing my faith. I know that's what I was born to do.

JIM

JIM IS so wonderful that he deserves his own chapter. Jim was a bit of a prodigy growing up. He's a freakishly good pianist with a great musical mind, someone who really hears music and understands the story within the sound. After *Project Lotus* I realized something else about him – he's one of the *good* guys: safe and warm company with an impeccable moral compass and a great sense of humour. He made me laugh when all I wanted to do was cry. So, I knew it would be good to take up his offer of writing together.

From day one there was something magical about writing with Jim. His talent and humility were the perfect combination. I never felt self-conscious about an idea. I never felt stupid singing out a half-cooked lyric or melody. We have the same rhythm of humour. If laughter's the best medicine then I always get a good dose from Jim and feel all the better for it.

We started writing together regularly. It was a totally natural progression. I felt keen to flex my writing muscles on something different, something that would never suit me as an artist.

One afternoon as I was hovering in the kitchen at the Steelworks I had a thought. The place was quiet. A couple of guys who had worked there in recent times had left. There was a free space upstairs. When I asked Eliot if I could station myself there he almost did a little skip. A big bear skip really.

'Philly! I'm so glad you just said that!' he said. It was a done deal. I would base myself there and get to work on music and future projects. In September I vacuumed the room and bought a candle for my desk.

It was a great move. I could now write with Jim at every given opportunity, or pop in and do backing vocals at the drop of a hat. We soon got busy penning pop songs. Before we knew it, Eliot was throwing projects at us. One of them was The Reason 4. They were a standout boy band (man band really) and they were crazily talented. After a couple of sessions with us material was flowing. It was so exciting. The boys had made a massive impression on the judges of the TV talent show *X Factor* by performing an a cappella arrangement of 'Fight for This Love' by Cheryl Cole. Cheryl loved it. The band made it to the boot camp stage of the competition and received lots of media attention (as well as attention from female fans). And now they were ready to release material. It was amazing to hear they were touring with Peter André. Songs we'd written with them were going down a storm – it was so exciting.

I went to see them do a showcase in London. Being the warm gentlemen that they are they gave us all a shout-out. It was magical. Not too long later, Eliot had a call from the *X Factor*. Gary Barlow had been appointed the new male judge after Simon's exit and Gary had requested Eliot (a friend since early Take That days) work alongside the talent.

It seemed amazing to me. The most profiled event in the country, the most talked about show on telly was coming for us – aiming at us with its big shiny arrow. A few sleeps later and Eliot was gone.

It was a big job for him, like *Project Lotus* on steroids. He had to be there most of the week living under the same roof as the contestants and working with them day in, day out. He began to work his band magic on a girl group known as Little Mix. Every week they shone. To me it was obvious that the Eliot Kennedy touch was on the show. He'd pop up in the behind-the-scenes bits regularly. I'm sure his phone exploded every time with, 'Just saw you on TV' texts.

Jim and I stayed at the Steelworks working on bits and pieces. I was still doing gigs. I felt a little flat though. We were spending a lot of time writing but I couldn't help but wonder if I was spending my time wisely. I wanted so badly to do something positive with my songwriting. It was tense not knowing what was around the corner. I began praying for some sort of sign. I felt I needed some kind of prod from God to tell me I was on track.

It happens every so often. It feels like a heavenly silence. No matter how often you've seen the tides change, it always feels like the silence lasts a lifetime. But when the silence breaks, it's as if a cool fountain is released over you, reminding you how glorious everything really is. That's what happened in a single week that December.

A Week of Signs

WE'D TRIMMED the tree. Steelworks was looking festive. Every few days we had word about how Eliot was doing. He was busy and stretched, but totally rocking the *X Factor*. The artists were growing week on week. It was so exciting to have a tiny glimpse behind the scenes to see how the contestants were doing.

We were keen to see the show for ourselves up close. But it seemed impossible. Even judges had a limited number of guest tickets due to audience capacity. So, I put any hopes of making it to the coveted final out of my mind.

In the meantime, Jim and I were beavering away on songs at the studio. Jim had been away on a couple of writing camps and seemed to be spending more and more time crafting songs. I hadn't done much in the way of writing for pop artists. So I was really excited when Eliot asked us to write with Sophie Habibis. She was a cracking singer who'd just left the show. I checked out her stats – ninety thousand followers on Twitter!

She was nothing but sweetness and grace. Just weeks earlier she'd been pulling pints in her local pub and she was grateful to have made the final ten. I think as a writing team, Sophie was a landmark for Jim and me. We penned four songs with her and they all felt special.

But it was just the beginning of a miracle storm. A week before the final I dropped into Steelworks to find a ticket for the final waiting for me at reception. It's hard to explain how that made me feel. It wasn't just the thrill of being at the event; it felt like a kiss from heaven after what had felt like a bit of a drought.

A couple of days later I was in town, pondering what to wear to the show, when I stopped to check Facebook (an occupational hazard). I had a message in my inbox. It was from a chap I'd met some months before. Our meeting had been a little fortuitous in itself. The night I went for my first dinner with Eliot he'd been behind the bar. He was managing the restaurant in fact. Eliot had spoken to him about his wife. She wasn't well. As they chatted, it came to light that she'd been struck down with a mystery illness and that they were struggling but coping. At the time their situation had really moved me. Months later, Michael had brought his wife to see a show I did with Eliot at the City Hall.

The message said:

> *Hello Philippa, how are you, you seem very busy? I have some PA gear: four speakers, amp and in-ear listening. I'm looking to find it a new home. It's a 3,500-watt rig and it's decent. I thought of selling it but then thought of you! Would this be any good to you or the church? Let me know – I want it to have a good new home. Michael*

Messages like that don't drop into my inbox every day. It was another kiss from heaven. I said I'd be happy to give the PA system a home and would love to see him. He dropped the gear at church one afternoon and we started chatting. His wife was still struggling, but they were staying upbeat. We chatted a little about church and he mentioned he might like to visit sometime.

MERRY CHRISTMAS

WHEN *X Factor* was over and Eliot came home, Steelworks lit up a little more. We finished the songs with Sophie and booked in some other writing sessions. The marvellous Craig Colton, who did well in the competition made plans to come up. I also had a call one day from Janet Devlin. Her pixyish Irish tones on the other end gave her away. She was keen to come and write with us. I enjoyed every part of that creative process. There's nothing like working with people who make you better at what you do. It makes me realize that the biggest miracle of all is people. Having people in your life who inspire you is priceless.

2012

DEAR READER, this brings us almost to the present day. The months that followed saw us writing with Craig, Janet and marvellous *Britain's Got Talent* runners-up, The Mend.

But the past year has also been a time for meeting and writing with long-term heroes of mine. The first time I heard the voice of Lucie Silvas it caught my attention. She was on MTV playing her piano and singing. Her soulful tones captured everything I admire in a singer. And she was a writer too. I recall sitting in my sister's front room watching Lucie's music video and thinking, 'That's the kind of artist I want to be.'

When Jim invited her up to write with us, I was over the moon. He'd worked with Lucie on a writing camp for *Project Lotus*. She'd known Eliot for years. It's nerve-racking working with your heroes. But when Jim said Lucie was super cool and totally amazing company he wasn't lying. We spent a good portion of the session talking about our lives and came out of it with a song we all really loved.

Another highlight was meeting Jennifer Paige. She had a huge hit in the nineties with her single, 'Crush'. The song was a number one worldwide and it made her a household name at the time. Even more pointedly, I had performed that song every single week on the club circuit. It was one of my favourites. I would step out onto smoky, working-men's-club stages and the comfort of that intro would put me in gear. I loved her nuances and vocal tone and tried hard to replicate it for the performances.

So when I found myself lunching with her in preparation for some writing sessions, I tried hard not to act star struck. She was gorgeous and her voice was every bit as wonderful in the writing room as on the record. What made things even more exciting was her character. We quickly became friends. She was a country girl at heart, with great manners and a beautiful, humble spirit.

Throughout the year, Roo and I went around the UK on our coffee shop tour. Every date was special. And meeting people, sharing this story and our songs has been incredible. Every show something golden happened – a connection with someone or a fabulous host family who would remind us that God uses anyone who is willing to serve, no matter what their gifts or calling.

God has continued his miracles. A real highlight was playing the Big Church Day Out festival. The love and support I felt from the audience there was touching. I felt so blessed and so comforted by God's ability to make these things happen.

Also at the event were Malcolm Down and his colleague Claire from Authentic Media. They had heard about me writing this book and wanted a quick chat. At the end of the show they came to speak to me and confirmed that they'd like to publish it. I was so excited.

Claire came up to see me in Sheffield for a final crunch meeting. We had to talk marketing and my plans to promote the book. It was a crucial conversation. The meeting went well and just as we were about to leave I spotted a familiar face in the restaurant.

To my amazement it was Baz – the same guy who had been there when I gave my life to the Lord. It was Baz who spoke at Alpha, convincing my dad to start the course. We went over to say hello. I looked at Claire as we left.

'See, this is it. That was a miracle! This is what happens every day. Baz could have been in any bar. But the guy that helped me get saved and began this *whole* story shows up at the meeting about it being published.'

I thought that was going to be the last miracle of the book. But it got better and better. Just a few weeks later, after months of wondering how I'd make the next CD, I managed to find an investor for my new album. The new songs I've been writing will see the light of day. Over the years I have prayed and prayed for the resources to enable me to make more music. God has far exceeded my expectations.

A Miracle in Progress

THERE'S A final miracle. This miracle will see the close of this book. There will be many more miracles in the future I'm sure. I know this because God is good. As it says in the book of Philippians (my favourite book because it has my name in the title) he is faithful to complete the work that he has started (see Philippians 1:6). He does more and more and more. We go from strength to strength.

Next Thursday is the first date of Lionel Richie's UK Tour. And I've somehow, through miracles and friendships and blessings, managed to get to be the tour support act. It's insane. I'm exploding inside. It feels like Christmas Eve times a billion. I can hardly believe that next Thursday I could be telling twelve thousand people that they are amazing! My hope and my objective is to share God's Spirit through this music and the evidence of transformation in my life. I want to fill those arenas with joy.

But we haven't signed the contract yet. So here's how I want to leave this paragraph. We need a final push from Jesus. We need his grace and favour to make sure all the threads come together in time. We need capital to secure the slot, and at this moment we don't have it together. So I'm going to invite you right into the centre of this final miracle.

Lord. I know you hear me. I know you care. I know because you've moved in so many ways in this little life of mine. You've saved my family. You've saved my soul. You've helped me become the person I want to be and more. You've done great things – miracles. And through my past suffering you've comforted people. I want to do more! Please God, help us secure that place. I know God that you have it written already. The plan is in place. The dates are secure in your will. I believe, I believe, I believe. I pray in Jesus' name that I would step out on that stage on Thursday, representing the heart of the King. God, may your will be done and your Kingdom come in Jesus' name. Amen.

Now. We wait.

EPILOGUE

Not the End

WELL, WHAT can I say? Thank you Lord. It all came together. There were hoops to jump through and mountains to climb. But we pulled it off. By God's grace and with the support of some wonderful people I got to open up for the Lionel Richie tour at eleven sold-out arenas across the UK!

I don't think I can convey what it felt like to walk out on stage with my acoustic guitar in front of twenty thousand people at the O2 arena. It was terrifying, but totally awesome. There was no safety net, no machine – just me and my songs. I realized pretty quickly that my own bottle wasn't sufficient. The first night at the NEC in Birmingham was enough to prove that to me.

What do you say to all those faces? How do you contend with a space that size? Within the blink of an eye the set was over and I was backstage again.

'Did I really just play to twelve thousand people?' I asked Joel. Both he and make-up artist Sara were sure it had been a success. But I felt like a novice again. I'd learned over the years to feel comfortable in most circumstances. I'd followed wonderful singers. I'd had to switch and change sets at short notice. I'd contended with dodgy PA systems and tough audiences. I thought I had enough experience to sink a battle-ship. But standing on stage before thousands who've never heard of you and would much rather be singing along to 'Easy like Sunday Morning' was a different kettle of fish altogether.

I came home to Sheffield after the first show and went round to the in-laws for dinner. My father-in-law Phil had some words of encouragement for me: David, the little shepherd boy had no armour. He had no rifle or cavalry to defeat Goliath, only his little slingshot. If David could bring down Goliath with a single rock, then I could jolly well rock the O2 with my Farida guitar. As the family prayed for me I absorbed their strength. There had never been more of a time to call upon my faith. This was a mountain. And on my own it seemed impossible. But I recalled the Scripture given me on the day of my baptism, 'I can do all things through Christ who strengthens me' (Philippians 4:13 NKJV).

The next show was the O2 arena. Even driving there made me nervous. The tall structure was visible miles away and with every inch closer, another butterfly popped into my stomach.

'How am I going to manage on stage if the very sight of the place makes me feel terrified?' I wondered, saying nothing to the team in the car.

The venue seemed endless. The view from stage was like that of the Starship Enterprise. The seats went so far up towards the ceiling it seemed likely people *would* be dancing on it. Backstage was endless too. As I finished the soundcheck I spotted a small blonde girl scuttling into the dressing room beside mine. I realized she was Pixie Lott.

Later as I was having my make-up done, the butterflies multiplying, I could hear her warming up with a vocal coach.

'Pixie Lott,' I thought. 'Doing scales just feet away.' It reminded me that my set was due to begin.

Moments later, Malcolm the stage manager came to the side of stage.

'We good to go?' he said, in his unnervingly mellow manner. This was someone who'd led Tina Turner, Eric Clapton, Elton John and indeed Lionel Richie to the stage many times. Now he was taking me! I braced myself on my four-inch heels (a desperate attempt to look bigger) and headed for the stage, warming up my voice with bubbles and trills all the way.

We went round the back of the stage and through the gap in the heavy black drapes. Once up the steps and behind the curtain I struggled to tune my guitar. Something about the hot room and my nervous plucking was throwing the strings out.

'Are you about ready?' said Malcolm. 'Remember girl, it's just a big coffee house.' I looked out at the packed arena. Twenty thousand people were shuffling into their seats. I looked at my tuner. Green lights all the way. It was time. I nodded to Malcolm.

He whispered into the radio on his jacket, 'OK, we're all set here. Lights down. Give me a little glow on stage.' As the lights went down, the audience began to cheer in anticipation.

'Hope they're not too mad that I'm not Lionel,' I thought as I trotted out from behind the curtain. The cheering lowered politely as I reached for my jack lead, plugging it in awkwardly.

'Please work, please work,' I thought as I braced myself to play the first chord of 'Happy in My Skin'. To my great relief, the sound filled the arena.

'Good evening London!' I said. And at that moment I was filled with peace, realizing that God brought me here. I didn't get here in my own strength. He'd called me to this place and would give me all I needed to fulfil the task. As I shared my songs I felt the audience warm. As I sang the song 'I Am Amazing' I felt my heart swell as I prayed internally that every person would know and believe that they were created for a purpose.

What a moment. What a victory. My mind recessed to where I'd been eight years before. I'd cried out for God's help in a small church in Sheffield. I had nothing left to give and no strength to try. I'd given up hope . . . almost. With the one spark of life that remained, I asked for Jesus to intervene and change the course of my life. After playing these shows I felt the smile in heaven. He'd known all along what was ahead if I could only trust him. I remember a message I'd had from youth leader Pete just months after I prayed that prayer, 'If you had any idea what God had in store for you, it would blow your mind.'

How right he'd been. As the Bible says, God can do more than we can ask or imagine:

Now to him who is able to do immeasurably more than all we ask or imagine, according to his power that is at work within us, to him be glory in the church and in Christ Jesus throughout all generations, for ever and ever! Amen (Ephesians 3:20).

**Philippa Hanna is represented by Storm5
Management**

Authentic

We trust you enjoyed reading this book
from Authentic Media. If you want to be
informed of any new titles from this author
and other exciting releases you can sign up
to the Authentic newsletter by contacting us:

By post:
Authentic Media
PO Box 6326
Bletchley
Milton Keynes
MK1 9GG

E-mail:
info@authenticmedia.co.uk

Follow us: